Yo
A Jeste

By John F

© John Pilkington 2022.

John Pilkington has asserted his rights under the Copyright, Design and Patents Act, 1988, to be identified as the author of this work.

First published in 2022 by Sharpe Books.

Table of Contents

AN ADDRESS TO THE GENTLE READER

ONE

TWO

THREE

FOUR

FIVE

SIX

SEVEN

EIGHT

NINE

TEN

ELEVEN

TWELVE

THIRTEEN

FOURTEEN

FIFTEEN

SIXTEEN

SEVENTEEN

EIGHTEEN

NINETEEN

TWENTY

TWENTY-ONE

TWENTY-TWO

TWENTY-THREE

TWENTY-FOUR

POSTREMO

AN ADDRESS TO THE GENTLE READER

Confiteo!

... is Latin for 'I confess'. That is how a certain scholar – the Queen's chaplain, no less – has urged me to begin. In the manner of a confession I write my history, if without hope of absolution. The same scholar – Mattheus by name – showed me his copy of Augustine's *Confessions*; the good bishop's book comforts and sustains him, he says, in his daily toil - though what does a man like him know of toil? Yet to humour him I looked at the first page and saw these words: *I will call to mind the impurity of my life past, and the unclean corruptions of my soul.* In the light of such fine intent, how can I not follow?

And so to my testimony. Whether it will be believed or even read by any mortal I cannot know – who but a hex can foresee anything? Before I begin, however, there are matters I should set forth. *In primis,* I am at times prone to embellishment, even flattery. How else would a runt like I have survived in the King's cold and windswept castle of Helsingor, where some bad-tempered courtier might aim a passing kick at me as if I were some cringing cur? I will alter that: I seldom cringed. Howled perhaps, in pain or rage, but I never truly abased myself – unless clowning for one's supper amounts to abasement. But stay, for I leap ahead of my tale.

Secundus, I'll admit that my anger has bettered me at times. I even grow angry with Mattheus, as gentle a creature as you may find anywhere. I once called him a Pious Little Turd. Naturally he forgave me: he is a true forgiver, a born kneeler at altars who believes I'm engaged in penning a repentance tract, for which he thanks his maker! At times I suspect Mattheus of aiming at some kind of martyrdom; then, deep-dyed sinners like myself are forever suspicious of the actions of good men. Yet who am I to condemn him, infirm and confined as I am - food for lice and fleas, and prey to memories that keep me from sleep?

A plague on them – I will look to my history. These are my words and no other's, for the setting down of which I'm beholden to no-one – no-one, that is, except the sweet boy: the beloved prince who raised me from an ignorant serf to a fellow of worth, by instructing his tutor to teach me my letters. By such a miracle, and to the envy of many, was I lifted beyond the dreams of the woman who bore me to attempt this task that lies ahead. Let the reader, if such exists, choose whether to follow me or no: I make bold enough to claim it will be worth the journey, to hear the tale of Yorick the jester. Whose true name was Erik.

Come if you will, and be entertained - even astonished.

ONE

Ecce aurora! Behold the dawn, in Latin. How else should a man commence his history, but at the dawning of his life? Mine came on a freezing winter's night (what other kind is there, in Denmark's winter?), when I emerged from the womb of Gitte the three-fingered, her cries the first sounds I would have heard as I tumbled into a tiny, dim-lit room crammed with women, most of whom had come from mere curiosity, having heard of the long and difficult birth. Though I knew nought of it at the time I was a puny infant – as sickly-looking, it was generally agreed, as had been seen in recent memory and, with the likelihood of my dying within the hour, it was also agreed that a priest should be summoned. But none could be found, or none who was willing to leave his bed and set forth in the cold to bless the bastard child of a lowly servant who was rumoured a whore to boot. Gitte, with the mangled hand and the squinty eye? Away with you, take her lifeless brat beyond the castle walls and dig a pit in the woods. To which I say, a pox on all priests – and in my first act of defiance, I confounded them all by bawling throughout the night.

Later, on hearing of what had transpired, my mother swore an oath: that as long as she breathed her child would thrive. And more: on his death he would be buried in sanctified ground alongside men and women of rank. Or so she told me when I was grown; and though she was prone to telling untruths when it suited her, I believe that was not one of them.

And what, some may ask, of the father of her offspring? Now there's a question, to which I have no ready answer. Not that I didn't wonder who he was, from the time I observed that other children seemed to have one and I didn't, aside from those whose sires had been lost to the misfortunes of war or sickness. I was marked out, that much was clear: the butt of gibes from the rascally boys of the castle and its surrounds, so that from the time I could walk I had to fight or... or fall, was I about to say? Well, sometimes there are other choices. This I learned from my very first teacher, the man who saved Gitte and her bastard son from likely starvation, being cast out as they were from the King's protection on account of his Queen's displeasure. Gitte, no sooner had she recovered from giving birth, was ordered to take herself across the Sund, quit the realm and beg succour among the Norwegians who were her forebears. So it was that her fate and mine might have been somewhat different had not a saviour appeared in the unlikely shape of Makan, the King's fool, who confounded everyone by asking his master's leave to take the wall-eyed drab and her child into his keeping.

What a stir that caused, at least for a week or two. The Queen was against it, of course, but on this occasion she was over-ruled. The King – Rorik, have I not named him yet? – King Rorik the Mighty would have his way. He adored his old *hofnar* Makan, who cheered him when others failed; who sat at his footstool when he returned from some warlike venture, pulled off his stinking boots and rubbed his tired feet, all the while cracking out jests until the monarch sniggered into his great beard. Makan, widowed for almost a decade, was in need of a woman to warm him at night, the King declared, and what if he chose Gitte the Unwanted? Hence, mother and child were installed in Makan's chamber in a quiet corner of Kronborg, with a view of the icy Sund. This became our home, and as time passed that squat, bow-legged man became - not my father, for he never pretended to that title; he was my almost-father, as well as my teacher. And the most important lesson he taught me was: do the unexpected.

'A bully comes at you with a mud-ball in his hand, about to sling it,' was one of the earliest things I recall him saying. 'So Erik, what can you do?'

'I can run, Makan.'

'He's bigger and faster than you, and will catch you with ease.'

'Then I can duck.'

'He'll be ready for that. When you duck, he'll merely lower his aim.'

'Then I am set for a face full of mud, Makan.'

'That is what he and everyone else expects. What is it, do you think, that no-one would expect you to do?'

Puzzled, I could only stare at him. It was a day in late summer, I recall, and we were in the King's fair garden picking up windblown fruit. Gitte would have been at work with the washerwomen, red of hands and face, her bad eye streaming as it always did. Rorik was off on some war-making expedition, hence his fool was free to spend his hours as he chose. As I watched, Makan stooped and picked up a soft brown apple, rotted and half-eaten by wasps. He lifted it and I flinched, thinking he would throw it, but instead he bent low, put on one of his 'looks' – he was a man of many faces – and squashed the pulpy fruit onto his own broad nose! I yelled with laughter.

'You mean I should seize the bully's hand and shove the mud into his own face!' I cried. But Makan wiped the mashed apple from his nose with one hand, raised the other one and wagged a finger at me.

'Wrong – you should do the opposite: seize his hand, and splatter yourself.'

I was dumbfounded. 'Do his cruel work for him? Why?'

'Think, Erik. If you did so, what would happen?'

I thought. 'He would laugh, and those who were watching would laugh too.'

'Indeed,' Makan nodded. 'So - you took the bully's power from him, and made it your own. You made everyone laugh, not he. Your only cost was a mudded face, which is soon washed. Whereas he would have no weapon.'

And there was my first lesson: to assess a likely course of events, then seek another way - the side-path that no-one has noticed. Look, then move swiftly; you stop moving, you die.

All in all, those were good years; it would be an untruth to say they were not. Between the two of them Gitte and Makan raised me to boyhood, and we were as well-bestowed as we dared to hope. My mother, bitter and strange as she was, never forgot Makan's saving of her and her child, and was a loyal wife to him in everything but avowed wedlock. Then, sin was a foreign notion to her as in many ways it was to Makan, who had come from rough-treated stable-boy to royal companion by way of plain stubbornness, a portion of cunning and a quicksilver wit which very few possessed. Though he had married when young, I learned later, it was because the woman was carrying his child and he would not forsake her. Even when the child died, and his wife turned into a whining drudge, he bore it; he was a man of loyalty such as I have rarely seen. Yet it was a relief, perhaps, when the woman succumbed to a fever and left him widowed. And though, when away from the King's presence Makan could be gloomy, his temper was soon allayed by a cup of Rhenish, or Gitte tugging him into bed; more likely both.

As I grew, I heard tales about Gitte which troubled me. How she was over-friendly with the hex who lived in an old fisher's hut by the Sund, and who was avoided by all but the desperate. How she had fled her home by the great lake of Vanern, because a price was on her head for some unknown crime. How she had followed armies and served soldiers and sutlers, drifting at last to Jutland where she found work as servant to a landsman, who sold her to one of Rorik's cooks for a flagon of mead, which is how she ended up at Kronborg. Gitte, who lost two fingers of her right hand to a drunken butcher's cleaver, for which the man lost his place – or so she told me; I confess I sometimes wondered at that.

I have said she was bitter, and when she flew into one of her rages I was more likely to bear the force of it than anyone else. That is, until there came the day when, as a lad of nine or ten years, I dared to defy her. It was an evening in high summer, and I was hot and thirsty from playing with my friend Trostann, the farrier's son. Entering the castle kitchens by the rear door I found Gitte in her apron, sweaty from her labours, coming fiercely towards me.

'Where have you been? You're too late for supper – get yourself to bed.'

'I need to drink first,' I said crossly.

'There's a jug of watered ale in the room. Leave some for Makan.'

'There's not,' I told her. 'I finished it this afternoon.'

She flew at me then, not so much for the words spoken but for the insolent manner in which I delivered them. As a rule I would have taken the blows, accepting my punishment before slinking off to recover or, if Makan was about, to seek solace in his presence. This day, however, was different; I know not why, save that there's a season for all things, and change will come – but away with such flummery. The truth is I felt a surge of anger that day in the hot kitchen, to startling effect for those who witnessed it. In short, I remembered what Makan had taught me and did the unexpected: dodged the blow, seized Gitte's hand – her good hand – and wrenched it aside, so sharply that she overbalanced. With a muffled curse she righted herself and would have lunged at me again – or so I thought. Instead, she stood looking down at me, hands at her sides, and an odd expression came over her.

'Drink from that pitcher, then,' she said, with a nod towards it. 'Then go to the room, but don't undress. Wait for me.'

This was unusual enough, but it was as nothing to what would follow on that summer's evening, which is burned deep in my memory. I recall assuaging my thirst under the eyes of the kitchen folk, before going to our room. There I waited, kicking my heels in my sweat-damp jerkin until it dried to my skin, mighty curious as to what would happen. Makan was at supper clowning for the King and his knights, their raucous laughter passing through walls from the High Hall to my ears, which after any normal tussle with Gitte would have been red and sore just now. Having naught to do but wait and wonder, I soon fell prey to fears about what punishment might be in store for me, and began hoping that Makan would be dismissed by his master and allowed to go to his quarters, though I soon gave up such a notion: Rorik would likely carouse all night, or until he fell asleep and had to be carried to his chamber under the disapproving eyes of his dour Queen. In truth I waited for perhaps an hour, until the light began to fade outside, and at last I heard the slap of Gitte's feet on the stones of the passage. As she came in I stood up, taut as a bowstring, and faced her as boldly as I dared. But all she said was: 'Put on your shoes and come with me.'

We went in silence through the corridors of Kronborg castle, keeping clear of the Hall whence came the sounds of revelry. Out by a narrow, unguarded door, past the outhouses and the stables, my curiosity growing all the while, especially when we fetched up at a postern gate in the castle wall which was seldom used. Without a sideways glance Gitte drew back the bolt and ushered me through, pulling the door shut behind us. Then she led me down the steep winding path to the Sund, which was spread before us in the gathering dusk, its ripples picking up the gleam of a sailor's sunset.

She did not take my hand; Gitte never showed affection for anyone save Makan. That she valued me in her own, crabbed way, however, and would fight tooth and nail to defend me, I seldom doubted, not even when she struck me for some slight or other. This night, filled with uncertainties as it had become, was no different in that regard. Wordless since we left the castle, she strode on in a determined manner, her coarse workaday frock flapping about her bare ankles as I made haste to keep up. Soon we were down by the shore where boats were tied up and seabirds shrieking, wisps of smoke issuing from the thatched huts of the fisher folk. People were about but Gitte ignored them and their stares, leading me past the last house, northwards along the strand where there was naught but rocks and the beating surf – whereupon I began to understand.

'Are you taking me to the hex?' I asked, my voice dry on a sudden.

She gave no answer.

'Mother?' With fear rising, I stopped. 'Are you?'

With a hiss of impatience, she was obliged to cease walking and face me.

'If I am, I have reason,' she said. 'And you've no cause to tremble like a rabbit – there's nothing to be afraid of.'

She waited, and I saw the challenge in her eye: the good blue one, that is. The other one, streaked brown and yellow like a hornet, stared off into the distance. She would not force me to go with her, I saw - the choice was mine: to run back to the castle and let myself in by the unbolted gate, or to follow her to the house of the hex, Edela. Last in the line, it was said, of a family of hexes who claimed descent from a god whose name was long forgotten. Edela, who lived alone and childless and was viewed with a mix of fear and dislike by her neighbours, even those who sought her counsel when no other course lay open to them. The hex, for her part, cared not a jot for she was fearless: vigorous and healthy beyond anyone of her years had the right to be, living apart with her goats and hens and her poor patch of stony land. Besides, she had the protection of King Rorik, who allowed her to live free provided she never came within his walls.

Well, I said no more to Gitte, merely picked up pace again and walked behind her, my ears filled with the sea's roar, though I confess my heart was aflutter. She'd said there was nothing to fear, yet I was unconvinced; I even began to suspect her of planning some terrible fate for me, in return for my defying her as I had – and the kind of punishment Edela could have meted out, should she wish it, was not to be dwelt on. So it was in this state of unease that I arrived at the hex's weathered old hut, its walls buttressed with beams hammered into the thin soil, its roof covered with turves and lashed down with withies. In a pen close by, her three goats stared at us with what looked like disdain. There was no smoke coming up through the roof, and an idle glance might have told that the place was empty. But the rough-planked door was open, and before it Gitte stopped and waited.

Nothing was said; a little behind her I stood rigid, struggling to rein in my fear. I had never been to Edela's house, only seen it from a distance; it was dangerous to be alone this far up the Sund, especially after dark. You might be beaten and robbed by outlaws, or even encounter the *draugen*: a dreadful sea monster, like a man but clad in seaweed, who would screech horribly. A breeze ruffled my collar and I shivered, hoping that our journey was fruitless; that the hex was away somewhere, so we could turn about and go home. But in that regard, my hopes were dashed. A figure I had only ever glimpsed from afar, tall and clad in rough peasant clothing, her grey hair tight-bound in long braids, appeared in the doorway as if she had been called.

'I thought it was time, Edela,' Gitte said, calm as you like. 'Here is the boy.'

With a sweep of her good hand she indicated the frightened Erik. Edela stepped out of her hut and regarded me in silence – and under the gaze of those black eyes, deep-sunk in a face burned nut-brown by sun and wind, I quaked. For once, I was bereft of speech.

'What are you called, boy?

Her voice, far from being that of a cracked old crone, was soft. She took another pace forward and my instinct was to step back, but I willed myself to stay.

'I'm Erik,' I mumbled.

'And what will you be, Erik?'

I was puzzled by that. No-one had ever asked me what I would do with my life: such choices were for nobles, not for the likes of Gitte and me. There beside the Sund with night falling, under the livid stare of this frightening woman, I was forced to reach into my ragbag of a mind and come up with a reply.

'I think I will be a *hofnar*, like Makan,' I managed, since no other answer was forthcoming.

Gitte looked at me then, with mingled surprise and what I hoped was approval; but one could never be sure with her. Edela said nothing for a while, then:

'You thought it was time?'

The question was for Gitte, who gave a shrug. 'He stood up to me. Soon he'll be set to work, and will forge his own path. I've done all I can for him.'

I gazed at her: it was the first I'd heard of being put to work, and I didn't like the sound of it. Kronborg and its precincts, the fields and woods, had been my playground since I could walk. It struck me then that despite the hardships every kingdom suffered – the threat of war, of plague and sickness, of fire and famine – I had always felt safe in Rorik's realm. And what was this from my mother, about her having done all she could for me?

'Come into the hut.'

Edela turned and went back indoors, seemingly without caring whether we followed or not. I was mighty afraid:

fearful tales were told of Edela's hut and what went on inside it. How nobody who entered was ever the same again; how she poisoned people who angered her, or put a curse on their families. Yet for myself, I say now that Edela was no such woman; that for all her odd ways she was a sage and a healer, who had been condemned for her heresy. She had laughed in the faces of priests, strong in her knowledge of lore that went back long before the coming of churchmen and in which, if truth be told, many of our people still believed. I know this, because I'm one who was touched by her.

We went inside and indeed there was, as Gitte said, nothing to be afraid of. There were jars and bunches of herbs, and dried fish hanging from the roof, and the place stank, but otherwise there were merely things to furnish her bare needs: a hearth with cooking pots, a pallet covered with an old sheepskin, upturned barrels and a table of unfinished boards, so cluttered that there was barely room to put down a stone. Edela, stooping a little, gestured Gitte to a barrel-seat and poured liquid from a heavy jug into two wooden cups.

'Will you drink, Erik?'

Gazing down at me, the hex held out the cup. I was aware of Gitte watching, though I wouldn't look at her; nor could I meet Edela's tar-black eyes. In the dim light I looked down at the liquid, which was flat and cloudy.

'Or do you think it'll turn you into a beast? A stoat, perhaps?'

I gulped, and took it from her steady hand; I guessed that this was some sort of challenge. 'I'd rather be a stallion,' I said without thinking – then jumped out of my skin, almost spilling the drink: Edela had thrown her head back and let out a barking laugh, more like a hound than a woman.

'Then, so you will,' she said. 'Now drink.'

I dared to take a sip – and was relieved to taste ale, of the plain sort brewed at the castle. Being thirsty I drank deeply, then drained the cup. After letting out a breath, I looked up and mumbled my thanks.

'Sit yourself,' Edela said. 'And let's see if we can tell what's coming to you.'

I did as she bade me; we all sat at her table as night fell, and stayed there an hour or more. After a while she bade Gitte leave us and sat with me alone, though I swear not a word passed her lips that I could hear. And when at last my mother and I left with a blazing torch to light our way homewards, one rumour at least of those spread about Edela would prove to be true: that the Erik who left her hut that summer's night was not the same Erik who had entered it, though he had no notion of it then. The passing of years would prove it so, and I'll speak of it when the time seems right.

But not yet, good reader; not yet.

TWO

The Kronborg stables: that's where I was put to work, within weeks of my encounter with the hex. I suppose it was a fitting enough start to my working life, if only because Makan had begun his in the same manner. But it was hard, I swear by my boots it was. I was the runt of the place: a beardless boy fit for naught but shovelling horse-shit, running errands and bearing the brunt of the rough language of the King's stablemen and the older boys. Even the horses sneered at me, and more than once I was caught on the shins by a flying hoof that appeared too well-aimed to be by mere chance. After a week I was not only bruised but twitchy, ever alert for a careless shove from one of my fellows, or a pail of water splashed over my feet. I see now that my wits were being honed from the start, forcing me to fashion some defence against the buffets I endured. Yet I was too dim-witted to know much, other than that I'd left childhood behind and was expected to stand on my own feet. I spoke of it one day, during a rare respite from my labours with Trostann the farrier's son, who worked with his father. Perhaps I overdid the bemoaning of my fate, for my friend soon lost patience.

'Stop your weaselling, Erik,' he said. 'It's no more than any lad endures when he enters a man's domain. You think I don't get shouted at for my slowness? You should ask others how it is – you've had it easier that most because you're Makan's boy. Few would want to risk his anger, seeing as he has the ear of the King himself. You should learn to fight better.'

He spoke aright. The notion of trying to fend off one of my stable-fellows by threatening to tell tales to Makan was unthinkable: I would be despised for it. I must indeed learn to fight better, I was thinking, when as if by design one of my chief tormentors appeared around the corner of the stable wall where we sat, perched on bales of straw. This thickset brute, Mogens by name, stopped and glowered at me.

'Slacking, as I thought. Get back to work, you little worm.'

Trostann made no move, since the barb wasn't aimed at him. But he turned to me, and I caught his meaning: was this a moment of importance? I had tensed from head to toe, yet reined in my instinct to get up and, at risk of a clout to the head, remained seated.

'Have you gone deaf?' Mogens stepped towards me. 'To work, I said.'

Fighting my own will, I stayed. Thoughts whirled in my head like birds, seeking a place to alight. In quick succession I pictured Edela telling me I would be a stallion – what had she meant? I saw Gitte's face, when I'd defied her in the kitchen – then I saw Makan squashing the rotten apple onto his nose, and I knew. I swallowed, then stuck a look of horror on my face and pointed at Mogens – that is, at his groin.

'By thunder, Mogens,' I said in a voice of awe. 'What's happened to your cock?'

The effect was striking: the sneer vanished, and a look of alarm appeared.

'What d'you mean?' He looked downwards.

'The swelling,' I said, still pointing. 'Can't you see?'

'What swelling?' He blinked, then tore at the waistband of his breeches and thrust his hand down... only to stop himself. Red-faced he looked up, as Trostann gave a shout of laughter.

'Cock-tugger!' he crowed. 'Is this where you always come, to pull your pod?'

Well: at once, Mogens roared and launched himself at us, but we were too quick for him. Trostann sprang one way, I another, evading his outstretched arms. He swung round but we were off, Trostann still laughing, I breathless and, though fearful of the consequences, filled with a new-found excitement. The unexpected was my weapon - and as with any weapon, I must learn how best to use it.

It would not be easy; I'd been lucky that time. Lucky that Trostann had been there to aid me; lucky that Mogens was a dull-witted oaf to fall for such a simple trick; lucky that he was unable to get at me for the rest of the day, since the King and his knights were riding out to hawking and there was too much to do. Yet he never clouted me again, perhaps fearing I would accuse him before the rest of the stable folk, of sloping off to tug his pod.

Whatever the measure of it, I believed I had gained a small victory, and I rejoiced. Makan saw my demeanour that night in the kitchens when, with me so dog-tired that I was falling asleep at my supper, he came to the corner where I sat and asked me how I fared.

'The work is hard, but I'm learning,' I told him.

'That's good.' He too was tired, I saw, and wore an expression that was unfamiliar; it looked like one of uncertainty. Doubt of any kind being not in Makan's nature, I was about to enquire how he too fared when he asked if I'd noticed that Gitte wasn't there. I had not, with half my mind still in the stables which had become my new home, in the daylight hours and often at night too.

'She's unwell,' he said. 'You'd best go to her when you've finished your supper.'

I blinked: Gitte was never unwell - the result, the gossips said, of her unholy friendship with the hex down at the Sund who had likely given her some means of warding off sickness. Or because of some curse that had brought about that terrible eye, and condemned her to eternal life; their heads were filled with such chaff. But I disliked the look on Makan's face and got up, asking him if he was coming too.

He shook his head. 'She wants to see you alone, Erik.'

I didn't like that either; there was foreboding in his voice. He had buried one wife - why should the death of another not follow? Uneasy now, I left him and went swiftly through the winding passages of Kronborg and up the stair to our room. On entering I expected to find Gitte abed, but she was sat in a corner with her legs splayed, sweating in the late summer evening, a half-empty cup by her side. As I drew near, she looked up.

'You remember the day we went to see Edela, and I told her I'd done all I could for you?' she said. 'They were not idle words, nor were they spoken in anger.'

I dropped to one knee before her, not knowing what to say. What surprised me further was, she lifted her good hand and

15

put it out; I could not recall a time when Gitte had raised it other than to hit me.

'There are things I would tell, while I can,' she said.

I took her hand but there was no grip; she was weak as a kitten. 'You're not dying,' I said, with no conviction at all. 'You can't.'

'I can,' came the reply. 'And I will.'

Her breath smelled bad and there was a limpness to her, as if her strength had drained through the floor. This was not the mother I knew; it was all wrong.

'How long have you been sick?' I asked. 'Does anyone know, beside Makan? I'll run for the healing-woman—'

'No.' She shook her head feebly. 'Only Edela could help, and she's forbidden.'

'Then what can I do?'

'You can shut your too-busy mouth and listen.'

I shut it and she withdrew her hand, letting it fall like a damp rag. With her good eye she regarded me for a while, then: 'You must be good to Makan and help him. He's older than you think, and has few years left.'

I swallowed, and managed a nod.

'So has Edela, come to that...' she looked away, and her mind seemed to be drifting a little. 'You should visit her again, when the time comes.'

'When what time comes?' I asked. 'How will I know?'

'You will, that's all,' she muttered. 'Now be silent while I talk.'

So I listened, sitting on the floor beside her as she spoke, for longer than she had ever spoken to me before. She told of the mother who died giving birth to her in distant Norway, of the father who blamed her for it and never spoke to her again, of the brothers who treated her cruelly so that she ran wild, and because of her squinty eye was said to be bewitched. She told of her wanderings before she came to Kronborg and of how King Rorik, for all his rough ways, was good enough to let her stay – until she found herself with child, and the Queen demanded she be banished. Having said this much she grew hoarse, so that I was torn by an urge to get help, yet loth to leave her side. I gestured to the cup, but she shook her head.

'Now you'll want to know of your father,' she said. 'What if I told you he was not of our sort, but one of high rank?'

My face must have fallen, whereupon she spoke harshly. 'You think I've lost my wits, do you? That no such man would want to rut with someone like me? Gitte with her mad eye... no, hold your tongue.'

I was about to bluster, but she stayed me. 'Think on this, Erik,' she went on, labouring for breath. 'That any man, even a king, may grow reckless when he's distracted, or drunk, or merely downcast. When his wife denies him his pleasures, shunning his embraces and driving him away to make war where none was needed, taking out his anger on his foes, falling to a savagery that quells even his own men. Such a man will, in the end, take solace wherever he finds it: behind a tree with some peasant girl, say – or even in a castle alcove of a night-time, should he chance upon a servant who was too frightened to do other than let him lift her smock and do his will. Can you not compass that?'

I stared at her. 'Is that why you were to be banished?' I blurted. 'Because King Rorik-'

'Did I speak his name? Did I say it was he?'

Gitte's good eye blazed at me, while my thoughts soared like swallows.

'I said any man may be driven to such, no more,' she went on. 'As for the banishment, that was the wish of others. If I had my suspicions, I never knew for certain who took me in the dark that night – and from the smell of strong drink that came off him, I doubt he knew much of it himself. Whatever the truth of it, it was Makan who took the blame. Now, dimwit, do you understand me?'

I believed I did; young as I was, I was not so ignorant of the ways of grown men and women that I could not piece things together. Finding herself in such a predicament, Gitte had given herself to the one man who could talk the King into letting her live at Kronborg and bear her child. I wondered then why she'd not found some means of ridding herself of her burden – surely Edela would have had such a remedy, as she was said to have helped others? Or why Gitte had not gone away to have her child, ditch-delivered as trulls practice, then sold it in secret... it was a dark turn my mind took that night, as the dusk closed in.

'Do you tell me that Makan believes he's my father?' I demanded. 'For he has never given me to think it.'

She hesitated, then: 'He did at first, but soon guessed the truth. You can't fool one who fools for his living. That he kept the matter private, as I begged him to, shows the measure of him. He's better than any in Kronborg... remember that.'

'But still...' I faltered. 'Why do you tell me of this now? How did you think I would deal with such knowledge? A stable-boy, with naught to expect but a life of hardship - even if Makan began his life in the same manner,' I added quickly, to forestall her. And when she merely gazed at me, I blundered on.

'Have you no answer? As when I told Edela that I would be a *hofnar* like Makan and you said nothing - were you laughing inside, knowing I was unworthy to follow him? Is that what you think, that I'm fit for naught but to labour like those shitted dolts in the stables-'

'Enough!'

The word snapped out, silencing me as always. Once it would have been accompanied by a blow; now all that followed was a sigh that rattled in her throat. She drew breath, then:

'I don't think that. You're fortunate - more than you know. Edela spoke of it, long before I took you to her. You'll prosper - though luck has its span, as does a life. Apply yourself, with every sinew you have. Listen to Makan, and you won't be a stable-boy for ever... that's all I can tell you.'

'Wait – what of Edela?' I persisted. 'What else did she say?'

But she closed her eyes; further questions would go unanswered. Bound up in a tangle of feelings, I sat and watched as the strains of living passed from her features, leaving them softer than I'd ever known. If you ignored her eye with its livid cast, you might even say she'd been pretty, once.

I stayed until long after dark, until Makan came at last, given leave by the King to attend Gitte who was dying as she had foretold; but he was already too late.

There are ghosts at Kronborg, and she is among them.

Nobody came to her graveside apart from Makan and I. Nor was it a proper burial, given Gitte's station: the Queen spoke against it, and the King did not press her. A priest was sent to do his office but did so with a poor grace, eager to be gone. Outside the castle walls, in a bare and lonely place set aside for those of low birth, Gitte was laid in the earth in a winding sheet, whereupon the gravedigger, Agnaar by name, began plying his spade the moment the prelate walked off. When Makan and I failed to move, he turned to us.

'Have you no jest, to send her on her way?' He enquired, his face blank as a wall. 'You being the Favoured Fool and all?'

Makan regarded him calmly – but I did not. Anger frothed up and, puny as I was, I might have run at the stone-faced wretch had not Makan grabbed me by the arm.

'Better a fool than a turd like you!' I cried, struggling to get free. 'Show some pity, if you can't summon any respect.'

'Respect?' The fellow regarded me in his dour fashion. 'It's too late for that, boy. She's but a feast for the worms now, like all the rest.'

'As will you be soon enough, Agnaar,' Makan said, speaking low.

The gravedigger shifted his gaze, leaned on his spade and spat on to the heap of earth. 'I'll see you in the ground, *Hofnar*, make no mistake about that,' he answered. To me he said: 'And likely my son will bury you some day, boy. Now, will you leave me to my work?'

We left him, Makan steering me away before I could let fly with some further retort. Yet I had no tears; nor would Gitte have had no patience with them. After we parted I went to the stables where the men left me alone to grieve, as they thought.

But they were wrong. Foremost in my mind was anger, a seething rage against everyone: my fellows, the castle servants with their gossip, the haughty Queen and even the

King, though I strove to forget what Gitte had told me about their relations more than ten years back: that was too much to bear.

And yet bear it I must, so that as weeks and months went by and the thought refused to leave me, I was forced to find a means to restrain it. It was too frightening, too powerful to dismiss; but by small, creeping shifts in my thinking I could push it aside. Since it seemed unlikely, if not preposterous, that the mighty King Rorik could be my true father, I reasoned, then it had to be mere fancy on Gitte's part. Her mind must have wandered, I told myself, even before she fell sick – perhaps long before she took me to see Edela. She had forged some illusion about her child's provenance, that had become hardened into fact. Makan, I vowed henceforth, would be my father: at the least I could carry out my mother's last wish, and try to be a good son to him. That was how my mind moved, back then.

I was entering my fighting years, which might have become a lifetime had matters not turned about as they did.

Just to think on it now, makes me giddy.

THREE

The boy Erik turned into a youth named Yorick, easily enough.

Grown into an able lad who, though prone to waspish grumbling, did his work well enough, I found that the blows and buffets of my early years diminished by steps, so that in time I became equal with the others. I slept in the hayloft now with the other boys, and took my meals at my work as often as in the kitchens. And I was trusted: to feed and exercise the best horses, even to saddle the King's mount when he went to hunt, or the Queen's fine palfrey when she rode it, though those times were few. She was a severe woman, grown gaunt with the years, spending more and more time closeted with her ladies. By contrast, as if to shame her with his vigour, Rorik ventured out more than ever, sometimes to distant corners of his kingdom where, we youngsters assumed, he took his manly pleasures. That the Queen slept apart from him in a great tapestried chamber was known to all, as it was known that Rorik sometimes stayed away for weeks on end, returning in better spirits than when he'd departed. Though he was getting old he was yet a king in every way, so that at word of his arrival we would scurry about to make everything ready. Which is how, over a matter of but a few days, I acquired the name I was known by ever after.

'Yo, Erik!' The stable-master would shout from the top of his lungs. 'Fetch the King's bridle and trappings – shift your arse!'

'Yo, Erik!' someone else calls. 'Have you not groomed the mare? Sharpen up!'

And 'Yo, Erik,' another might say. 'Isn't it time you split the whisker with young Ragnhild, and made a man of yourself?'

That last question could draw laughter from every corner of the stables, and to my shame I would blush like a girl. And in truth it was a girl that was the cause of my disquiet then: the maid Ragnhild, somewhat older than myself. I noticed her from her first day in the kitchens where she'd been sent by her family who, seeing her growing plumpness, decided she should lose it by treading the stone floors of Kronborg from dawn to night-time. She was not over-pretty, yet she was lively and could fend off any slur with a smile and a riposte of her own. Soon after her arrival I saw her bend to pluck herbs in the kitchen garden, her ample rump producing a breeches-tightening response – and *confiteo*: I tugged myself off to sleep that night, and a good number of nights thereafter. And my gaze having strayed in Ragnhild's direction more often than I knew, I suffered taunts by the day until I could stand it no longer.

'Yo, Erik - won't she let you put it in, then?'

That was Mogens: the bully who had once shoved me about, but nowadays aimed assaults via his flabby mouth. He was grown fat and heavy-limbed, dripping with sweat most of the time, and had lost none of his meanness.

'From what I've seen there's room enough for two in there, wouldn't you say?' He rumbled on, grinning like a frog. 'Do you need any help?'

Laughter followed, but it died away swiftly: I was stung into action, and every man and boy saw it. It would not be the first time I'd come to blows: though slight of build I was always ready with my bunched fists, having taken Trostann's words to heart those years ago and learned from him – though not from Makan: his ways were not yet mine. Instead of doing the unexpected, I seldom failed to do the opposite: rising to a challenge like a fish to the bait and getting into another fight which, like as not, would leave me as bruised and blooded as my opponent. This day in early autumn would likely be no different, it was assumed by all - including the stable-master, Asel, who came striding over to us.

'I'm weary of you two, with your griping at each other,' he growled at Mogens and me. 'Go outside and settle it, once and for all. Whoever comes back in first is the winner, and let that be the end of it. Off with you!'

Under the eyes of everyone we went out, and I hoped Mogens was now regretting it as much as I was. He had strength and weight, and a hide like a boar's, but I was quick and agile, with bony knuckles and a habit of kicking out, learned - I swear it – from the ponies. Nobody followed: it was our business. Out to the yard we went, with its heaps of straw and dung, into a chill breeze. I allowed Mogens to go first, letting him see me close the door firmly behind us. Wary as wildcats, we stepped across the cobbles and squared up.

'I owe you a mashing,' I said, sounding a good deal more confident than I felt; I was a player at heart, though I barely knew it. 'When you fall, mind you don't land in the shit.'

'Mind yourself,' Mogens retorted. 'In the shit's where you will be.'

I crouched, assuming a baleful glare. 'Go to it then,' I said, 'so I can put you on your arse and get back to work.'

'You first,' was the snarled reply, him going into a crouch of his own, as far as his fat legs would allow it.

'No, you,' I said – and at sound of my own words, laughter spluttered up. 'I wouldn't want to take advantage of your slowness,' I went on. To which Mogens scowled - and tipped the whole business into a comedy. I followed the words with a laugh, doubling over at sight of his face full of righteous anger.

'What's funny?' Still scowling, he advanced a step. 'I'll knock that smirk off you, runt…'

'No, please!' In feigned terror I stepped back. 'You're such a warrior… isn't he?' I added, turning sharply and directing my question to the top of the stable wall.

It worked, so easily that I smile now to think on it. Mogens jerked round, looking for the non-existent watcher atop the wall - whereupon I hit him with my best haymaker, hard as I could on his exposed cheek. He staggered, with shock more than pain, then rotated his fat frame in my direction. Whereupon for good measure I laid in with a couple of blows to his stomach, another to his jaw and a finisher to his pudgy nose.

It was enough: blood welled and the poor fellow wheezed and sagged, a look of such astonishment on his features I almost laughed again. Since his knees looked as if they were about to fold, I gave him a backwards shove with both hands, putting him down flat on his well-padded rump. Mogens wasn't suited to combat, I saw – or at the least, not with a budding tumbler like Erik. A short time passed while I debated whether or not to let him get up, to give him another chance. But when I saw his ugly features, contorted with rage and pity for himself, I decided against it. With a shrug I left him and went back inside the stable – and stopped in my tracks at the cheer that went up.

There they stood, men and boys, saluting my victory. And though I knew I barely deserved it, yet I was thrilled in a way I'd never known – and more, it was another turning in the path. I stood in silence, as Asel came forward and clapped me on the shoulder.

'Yo, Erik - you've just won me five *pennings*. Have a drink.'

Grinning, he offered me a mug, drawn from the barrel which was kept for hot days when we needed to slake our thirst, and which I'd thought was empty. I took it and drank: the ale was sour as ditch-water, but it could have been the finest wine. I drained it, and held it aloft to another cheer. Whereupon, calling to mind a trick Makan had once shown me, I stood on my hands and walked a few paces, beating my heels together, which drew loud applause.

'Yo, Erik - Yorick!' Someone shouted. 'Yorick for ever!'

And I was Yorick thereafter; and shall be for the rest of my days.

Well: it was some time after my easy victory over Mogens that a truly momentous event came about, which I'm eager to relate. I was a strutting youth of around eighteen years by then: too cocksure for one of my station and, in the general way of things, likely due for a fall – were it not for my luck, which had held good until now. But first, let me bid farewell to Mogens who was sullen thereafter, and never spoke to me again.

So - to the Momentous Event. Word, it seemed, had spread about Kronborg that young Yorick was a lad of some merit, with a restless wit that might be put to better purpose than stable work. I know now, of course, that it was Makan who had been stoking such gossip, dropping a word in the King's ear when he could. And that autumn, when Rorik's troupe of players returned after a summer of performing in Jutland for the King's friend Lord Gerwendil, Makan saw his chance. He first begged the King's leave, choosing the right moment with his practised eye, and won consent. Then over a jug of strong ale he persuaded the leading player, Eghil by name, to try me – and if I proved worthy, to take me into his protection and teach me his craft. In this way, my course was set.

It was a miracle, or the closest thing to one I knew of. It would lift me from a life of bonded and blistered labour, with its sweaty summers and freezing winters, to a world of feasting and banquets where I would entertain the highest in Denmark. And if it set me apart from my plain, honest fellows – even Trostann, the staunchest friend a boy could have had – it was to bring me into the candlelit glow of another circle: one of elegance and beauty, and fine clothes and jewels; of rich food and wines, of clever speech and merriment. *Confiteo*: with what shreds of humility I possess, I give thanks to those who brought it about – to Makan of course, but also to the hex Edela, who made me compass a better life.

I would see her once more, and once only; yet I stray again.

Well now - the King's players. The players were a ragged collection of spirited souls who, under a different monarch's rule, might have been scorned and shunned as madmen and confined in some prison, or sold into slavery to be beaten for the rest of their days. Rorik, however, was gifted not only with a streak of kindness but with a shrewd eye for any man's ability, and a willingness to let him prove his worth – which included those who could amuse him and his Court at the great feasts of which he was so fond. And he gave his consent to Makan, which is how Yorick found himself plucked from the stables and brought to the outhouse where the players lived and practised their skills away from prying eyes, honing them to fitness for performance in the High Hall before the King and his nobles. It was to be a baptism, nothing less - though not one of fire: my first experience of life as a prentice in Eghil's troupe was to be drenched with water.

'Welcome, good Yorick,' our leader intoned in a voice of great solemnity, as I knelt to receive a pitcher of icy well-water poured over my head. 'I will first baptise thee into the company of fools, the seers of our age who are privy to the secret of life: that the world is mad, and all that moves upon it. Pledge allegiance now to the craft of foolery, where playing and mockery are the proper responses to everything. Have you aught to say, before you rise?'

Gasping and dripping, I looked up into my new master's handsome face with its neat-cut beard, his expression one of mock severity. The other players were watching closely: it was a trial, naturally – and all I could think of were those words of Makan's, from long ago.

'I say, do the unexpected!' I spluttered. 'All is in motion, and when you stop moving you die. So there but two sorts on this earth: the quick and the dead!'

A silence followed, and my spirits sank. As I got to my feet I felt their eyes on me: Niall who juggled and conjured, drawing live worms and spiders from his mouth, even a living snake; wiry Freybjorn who could stop his breathing - even stop his heart, it was said – and play a corpse, or a ghost, or a murderous villain; fair-faced Sveinn who could draw a tune from any instrument, and sing sweetly and play the maiden, be it washerwoman or princess. And Eghil: the best in everything from low comedy to high tragedy, frowning upon me as if about to pass judgement, which at last he did.

'That's wisdom enough - for a stable-lad,' he murmured. 'But what can you do? Show us.'

I stared at him, my mind a whirligig. What could I do? Thinking fast, I dropped to my hands and walked back and forth, regretting that I could not fart a hunting call while doing so as Makan could. After making a few circles, I stood up.

The result was another stony silence.

'Nothing further?' Eghil asked gravely.

I gulped and glanced at the others, none of whom had yet uttered a word. Would the company reject me? I knew nothing then of the ways of these folk who lived by a different code, who seemed not to know their proper place but dared to mock lords and knights, even kings. Who cursed and spat like other men, yet in the next moment could speak verse and declaim speeches as if they were high-born. I had much to learn - and had I given in to my weakest instincts just then, I might have run back to the stable and begged Asel to set me to work again. But one spoke up, and it was Sveinn.

'I'll try him.'

He came forward: a slender young man with no beard, somewhat garishly dressed, stepping lightly. As he approached, I stiffened. And when he came close – uncomfortably so – I was all set to parry a blow, until he confounded me by doing the truly unexpected: in short, he took my face in his hands and kissed me on the mouth!

By thunder, how aghast and amazed was Yorick. What should he do? he wondered, turning scarlet with embarrassment. What sort of a trial was this - was I expected to kiss the fellow back as if he were a maid, or hammer him into the ground? Speechless, I stood undecided until the silence was broken by a shout of laughter from all sides, followed by loud applause.

'What faces he has!' Eghil exclaimed. 'A whole store of them, and in such quick succession.' He peered at me. 'But can he feign them? Come, boy - show your anger. Show me your outrage at Sveinn, who stole a kiss so shamelessly.'

Well, that was easy enough, for there was little feigning to do now that I was recovering from the assault. I seized the pretty young fellow by his collar with one hand and drew back the other in readiness to blacken his eye, scowling with rage. Though I knew enough to hold back - especially when Sveinn merely smiled at me; when he pinched my cheek, however, I was at some pains to restrain myself. There was more laughter from the others, and it was a relief when Eghil clapped his hands, loud as a thunder-crack.

'Good! Now release our friend, pray, before you tear his jerkin. It's the only one he has.'

I did so, feeling oddly ashamed. I avoided their eyes, thinking that perhaps this was not the place for me after all: that I had fooled myself into believing I could pass so easily from my old life. I flinched when Sveinn tapped me on the shoulder – but turned to find him extending his hand, his smile one of true warmth.

I took it and was held firmly, whereupon with mingled surprise and relief I returned his grip. They surrounded me then, the entire company: Eghil, Niall, Freybjorn and Sveinn, offering handshakes and slaps on the back. Soon my anger and shame melted away, leaving me an empty vessel – or should I say wax, that is fit for any impression? In gratitude and wonder I stood among them, warmed by their bodies, as I'd never stood among men before. Then and there I formed my resolve: that somehow, I would make this my work; make Makan proud of me - and Gitte too, if her spirit could but see. I would watch and learn, and not fear to be laughed at.

I was Yorick, who would one day become the King's *scurra*; that's jester, in Latin.

FOUR

It was soon known throughout Kronborg - and beyond, to the town of Helsingor which lay under its protection – that the King's players had increased their number by one: Gitte's son, the stable-lad who'd once been to the hex, who was quick to anger and, it was generally agreed, could benefit from being taken down a peg or two. Here was the collapse of my first illusion: that as a player I would be admired and respected, set apart for my skills. Wrong, most woefully wrong: I was yet a servant, no higher than the rest, and in some people's eyes lesser than most. Eghil's troupe, I discovered, were looked at askance because they did no real work: grew no crops, tended no flocks, made nothing except prize fools of themselves before the King and his company, and were yet rewarded for it.

Priests despised them, of course: men pretending to be women was unholy, as was the disrespectful manner in which the players disported themselves. Other servants envied them their easy life: their own outhouse where I too now slept, the colourful attire they wore, the tossed coins they garnered from carousing noblemen - and more, the favours they were said to receive from certain ladies who admired them. Though not the Queen, it must be said: their very presence was a trial to her. Not once, in all my time at Kronborg, did I see her crack a smile; and when Eghil's men played in the High Hall she would excuse herself, not troubling to hide her displeasure.

No: Yorick had much to learn, and this was but the start. So that after a bruising time of being taught simple skills, like how to fall on my arse without hurting, I sought out Makan. It was late at night, winter was upon us, and he was in the old chamber where he now lived alone, with Gitte's presence but a memory. Before his small fire of pine cones he bade me sit, and asked me a question.

'Has the *mareridt* come to torment you, as it does me?'

I was taken aback by that. Like everyone else I knew of the *mareridt*: the mare which came to people in their sleep, sitting

29

on their bodies and giving them fearful dreams. Not being prey to such myself, I shook my head.

'That's well.' He stared into the fire, and on a sudden I was struck by how old he looked. *He's older than you think* Gitte had told me, when she lay dying.

'What is it that torments you?' I ventured. It felt strange, inviting my almost-father to confide in me: wise Makan, who had raised me and taught me so much. The troubling thought arose that this had some bearing on Gitte, at which moment he looked round.

'Not her, if that's how your mind moves. She's at peace... or I hope she is.'

'I believe she is too,' I said, though I was far from certain of it.

'I never asked what she said to you, that night,' Makan said then, making me uneasy with his stare. 'But I know what hopes she had for you. We'd lie awake when you were a babe and talk as you slept - there were sides to her you never saw, Erik'. He used my boyhood name, and would until the day he died. 'Don't think too harshly of her, who was so hard on you.'

'I don't,' I lied, which was foolish of me. 'She knew no better-'

'Stop that.'

I fell silent; no one could lie to Makan. Wearing his teaching face, which I had not seen in years, he frowned upon me. 'I see your anger, and I know whence it comes. You must curb it, turn its power to your own use as I told you long ago. You're a player now – learn from Eghil, and learn fast.'

'I am... I will,' I answered, falling into a child-like desire to please him. 'It's a wondrous chance for me - and I know it was you who brought it about.'

Impatiently he dismissed the matter. 'It's late... what'll we talk of? Have you got to know Niall, who's called by the Saxons *fristalles* – meaning "eats everything"?'

'I have,' I said, glad to move to another topic. 'He told me he was once a soldier, who broke up and ate his cuirass for a bet before they threw him out. I find that hard to believe.'

'As did I, once,' Makan said. 'Now I'm quite ready to believe it. Our age is one of wonder... my regret is that I shan't live long enough to know much more.'

'You?' I was unwilling to follow him down this gloomy byway. 'You're nimble as a lamb – and strong, as when you used to carry me on your back. I'd wager five *pennings* you could do so yet.'

'So, you're a gambler nowadays?' he enquired, straight-faced. 'A true fool indeed.'

'Would that I were,' I said with a rueful smile. 'To my fellows I'm a raw prentice who can barely juggle three balls, let alone make himself a ghost as Freybjorn can, or sing like Sveinn, or declaim fine speeches like Eghil...'

I broke off, for Makan was shaking his head. 'But that's not why you're with them,' he said. 'Your task is not to copy the others. Each man has his skill – what need have they for another Freybjorn or Sveinn? You must make your own path – become your own kind of fool. Do you not see that?'

'Do the unexpected?' I enquired, to which he nodded eagerly.

'It's the key to making folk laugh – the way to triumph in every endeavour. How else do you think the King has defeated his enemies, and kept such a hold on his realm? Because he knows others think he'll do *this* - so he does *that* instead.'

Our eyes met, and I was heartened: I saw not only love, but respect in Makan's gaze – and hence I was confounded by his next words.

'And it's the King who holds your future in his hands, Erik. Study how to divert him and change his humours, as I did. For when I'm laid in my grave – shovelled into it, like as not, by that old mole Agnaar who'll smile as he does it – who else is there to fill my place? That's who you can be, even if you'd never dreamed of such. Do you understand?'

Confiteo: at that my heart gave a thud. I told myself it was a crack from the fire that startled me; more, I wondered whether Makan was making fancies of what he wished to see, rather than what was possible. But when I turned the matter about that night, lying sleepless on my pallet while my fellows snored about me, I knew that wasn't so. For some time – likely for longer than I knew – Makan had nurtured the hope that I would follow him and become the King's fool in my turn: spend my days with Rorik the Mighty, sitting at his feet and soothing his cares - even hearing his whispered confidences, as it was said Makan did. And I recalled the answer I'd given to the hex Edela years before, when she asked me what I would be. Had she seen it writ in my palm that night, yet not told me of it?

Confiteo: the notion filled me not with joy, as it should have, but with fear. That Yorik, the bastard son of Gitte the Disfavoured, fit for nothing but the humblest of lives, could aspire to such a place was hard to compass; even now I think on it with amazement.

Midwinter came, and it was Yuletide, with feasting and fooling enough to fill my days and nights. I was now – I write it with pride – on my way to becoming a passable clown: a foil for the swift-tongued jests of Sveinn and Eghil, an admiring helper to Niall as he swallowed impossible objects like bodkins and spoons, bringing gasps of astonishment when he drew them out. The live snake, too: his name was Jofurr, and he was Niall's constant companion. He was russet coloured with a dark stripe down his back, he came from some land to the south of Denmark and his bite was said to be deadly. What nobody knew, outside of our company, was that his fangs had been pulled long ago, rendering him harmless.

Niall would sit with Jofurr curled about his neck, trading tales with Eghil about their days spent wandering countries beyond our own: of bedding maidens in barns and hayricks, or fleeing from angry mobs who accused them of thieving or even of witchery. They bore the marks of their exploits: Eghil a livid scar on his side, Niall the welts on his back from a whipping. Freybjorn too, bore similar marks: as a youth he had offended his master and fled, falling in with travelling jugglers before fetching up in Helsingor. While Sveinn…

Sveinn was an orphan who, it was generally agreed, was blessed: endowed with such a sweet singing voice, he could have charmed a hangman into taking his place. And after hearing him stun the entire company of the King's Hall to silence, who is Yorick to deny it?

These men were more than companions: they were my family. I ate and slept alongside them, learned from them, shared laughter and hardship, as when King Rorik went away and we were left to shift for ourselves, unpaid and often unwanted. I had discovered by now how precarious was the life of such folk, who entertain not merely for their supper but for their very survival. Hence, I became resolved to heed Makan's words and get myself noticed; to catch the King's eye, and make myself desirable as his fool.

And so I come to the time of my rising – the double nature of which term might amuse some, but would doubtless fill others (like the worthy chaplain Mattheus) with disapproval. Well, I say - away with piety and prudery! Let me set down the next turn of events, which bear on matters of the flesh - and I will speak in time of certain women. Yet first, I must step aside and tell of a gentle maid who earned my gratitude and affection: who took this green youth and – in the words of his fellows – allowed him to Split the Whisker.

It was long overdue, a fact of which I was made shamefully aware by the men of Eghil's troupe, who were amused to learn of this tardiness on my part. To say that they were all well-versed in the lore of seduction and its blissful fulfilment, of the landscape of the female form, not to say the mingling of pleasure and peril which accompanies such, would be an injustice. Even the youngest, Sveinn, was a master of what Eghil, with mock-haughtiness, would refer to as Puissant Coition. Though Sveinn – I may tell of it, for he's safe from censure now – was singular among them, being wont to lie with men as readily as with women; I never forgot the kiss on the lips he gave me, that day I was baptised into the company. Rumours flew about Kronborg with regard to Sveinn's activities, which only the King's protection prevented from becoming real danger. Or perhaps not only that, but the things Sveinn could tell of certain worthies known to him - even, he claimed, the Bishop of Roskilde. But I will hold to my purpose, and tell of my own arrival at the Grove of Pleasure.

Most vividly do I recall that night of performance in the High Hall, warmed by a huge fire, bedecked with green boughs and glittering with the light of many candles; the night when, before a great host of guests, our company sang and clowned, and at the last played the dramatic interlude the *Hanrej*, or the *Jaloux Mand - The Jealous Husband*. It was a favourite of Eghil's, who ranted with great passion as the lord whose wife cuckolds him with his steward. Freybjorn, employing his wickedest leer and drawing angry mutterings from the watchers, was the lusty steward; Sveinn, of course, the pliant Lady. Niall too did us proud, as the scheming counsellor who helps the Lady arrange her trysts... and Yorick?

Yorick – in a headpiece of dyed horsehair, a padded smock reaching to his heels and dainty slippers on his feet – played the Lady's simpering maidservant. And mighty grateful was he for the wheat flour that whitened his face, since it hid a blush that, had it been exposed, would have brought calls for a physician to stem the seeming flux of blood to his head.

And yet, when our play was done I tasted glory that night: the thrill of loud applause and cries of approval, the look of contentment on Rorik's features – and most of all, the glow of pride on the face of Makan, who stood close to the King. The noise rang to the roof-beams, and carried on as we made our bows, hearts lifted with pleasure and – truth to tell - relief. The King tossed a full purse to a servant, who brought it to Eghil, who bowed again in thanks. When we stood to relish the cheers even Yorick was smiling through his layer of flour, not to say sweating like a packhorse. Coins were thrown, the company snatching them with practised skill, Freybjorn holding out his hat to catch those they missed. Whereupon, looking about at the splendour, the men clad in their fine clothes and gold chains, their wives in silken gowns and jewels, I saw something else - something that sobered me.

In short, I learned in that moment that the tales were true: that from the brazen looks, the sidelong glances filled with meaning on the faces of sundry ladies seated about the Hall – older ones as well as young - any one of us might have sated his lust that very night, had he found a secluded place in which to do it. Even Eghil, grey-haired as he was. Nor were those admiring smiles lost on my fellows, who exchanged private looks. And it was when we at last left the scene of our triumph, that Eghil came up beside me and spoke low.

'This is your night, Yorick. Set your eyes on the pretty servant with the fox-red hair, standing by the door. She's been watching you – did you not notice?'

Well, I ducked my head: for all my insolence back then, when it came to matters of the other sex I was yet tongue-tied. But I slowed my pace and forced myself to look at the maid in question – and drew breath.

It was Dorethe: the most recent arrival at King Rorik's kitchens - and the fairest, it was said, in living memory. I stared... could it be true? Sweet, slender Dorethe, who turned heads wherever she went? Who was now the cause of half the men at Kronborg, Yorick among them, tugging themselves off to sleep more often than they dared admit? The same Dorethe who yet remained chaste, and seemingly unassailable? Yet here she was, serving at the feast, holding a jug of frothing ale and looking straight at Yorick in his woman's attire, skirts swishing about his ankles.

In disbelief, yet with a rush of mingled hope and desire, I left the others and moved towards her - and when I struggled to find the words, she forestalled me.

'In the brewing-house, in an hour. Or it might be two... wait there.'

Upon which she moved calmly away, taking ale to the revellers.

Confiteo: what followed was two hours of anticipation, tempered with torment.

In pitch dark, in the cold of the deserted brewing-house, I sat huddled in a nest made of sacking, caught betwixt fear and excitement: fear that I would fail to achieve my aim, yet feverish with desire. For this would be no lonely tugging of my poor virginal cock: I was about to experience intimacy with another.

Hence, I waited. The noise of revelry from the High Hall drifted my way, punctuated with bursts of laughter: Makan was at work, drawing on his stock of rhymes and jests. The King being in good spirits, carousing could last until dawn, which gave me cause for alarm that Dorethe would be unable to get away to keep our tryst. As time drew on, and I was forced to wrap myself about with empty sacks to keep out the cold, I grew downhearted: perhaps it would not be *my night* after all, as Eghil had foretold. A wind got up, blowing in from the Sund and rattling the shutters of the old building, so that I shivered and cursed – then in the next moment, caught my breath. There were footsteps, the squeal of the latch as the door opened, letting in a chink of light. A shadow passed fleetingly through the gap, the door closed quickly, then came a voice.

'Yorick – are you there?'

With a shiver, I answered. 'I'm here... I've made a couch of sacking.'

A rustle of skirts followed as she stepped towards me, groping her way in the dark. I got to my feet, letting the covers fall away - and only then did I remember that my face was still whited with flour! Thanking the darkness that she couldn't see, I wiped myself hurriedly with a sleeve, then drew a sharp breath as a hand came out of the gloom to touch my shoulder. I took hold of it, pressing it between both of mine, whereupon she flinched.

'You're cold as ice.'

'We'll soon warm ourselves,' I said, trying to sound like a man of knowledge. 'Will you sit down here, and...'

'And what?' Her voice sounded strange in the muffled dark, the two of us alone together as we'd never been. Lost for a reply, I merely kept hold of her hand until, to my abashment, she gave a low chuckle.

'What did you think we would do here?' She went on. 'Tell me.'

Whereupon it hit me like a thunderbolt, making me drop her hand as if it were a live coal.

'By the gods,' I breathed, 'you're not Dorethe!'

And at once a new fear sprang up: that this was some jest contrived by my fellow players! It would not be beyond them – I could even envisage the door flying open to reveal the entire company standing there, roaring with laughter. They scorn me, I thought – and worse, news of my failings would be spread about the kitchen next morning, and thence to the whole of Kronborg... in dismay I shivered again, whereupon:

'Indeed, I'm not,' came the voice. 'Don't you know who I am?' Upon which realisation followed, giving me another jolt.

'Ragnhild?'

The answer was another throaty chuckle that served for assent – and I was speechless. In my blind desire for Dorethe, now the object of my lustful fancies, I had barely given plump Ragnhild a thought of late. Yet here she was...

'So – have you come to mock me?' I blurted.

A pause, then: 'I would never do so, Yorick.'

Out of the blackness, her hand found mine again and clasped it. 'Say that I was Dorethe – do you wish to imagine it?' She asked. 'And in this dark, had I not spoken, would you know otherwise? I'll ask you again: what did you think to do here?'

'In truth, I didn't allow myself to think very much,' I answered. 'Yet I hoped...'

'Well then, so did I,' Ragnhild said softly. 'And I've waited long enough.'

And without warning she kissed me on the mouth: a warm, glorious kiss that sent a thrill through my loins, leaving me breathless.

'Now let's lie in this nest you've made,' she said. 'And take off that foolish frock... I've no wish to be smacked in the eye by a pair of false dugs. What are they made of?'

'Wads of bombast,' I said, breathing hard as I released her hand from mine. 'And I loathe them, as I loathe taking the maid's part-'

I yelped: to my shock and delight her hand had gone straight to my crotch, grasping my parts through the thin taffeta of the smock. Whereupon I fumbled at her clothing – and both fear and disappointment melted away as my manhood rose to a mighty hardness. Falling to my knees, pulling her down with me, I whispered her name in the dark, feeling her shiver when my cold hands caressed her. Quickly - and somewhat expertly - she shed her clothing, getting down beside me on the coarse sacking. In a fever of desire I grabbed her loose breasts, mauling and mouthing them like a babe as she stretched out beside me, whereupon:

'Don't take too long about that,' she said. 'I run like an old stream... will you put your hand where it matters, or must I guide you?'

Well *satis!* – that means 'enough' in Latin. For by my bones, I've a rod in my breeches now just to think on it. There's my honest account of how Yorick took farewell of his youthful self and entered the Grove of Pleasure, in wonder and gratitude, and in giddy silence. And though odorous and overgrown, it was a true garden of bliss, where I longed to remain forever. Would that it were so; but as any man knows its joys are fleeting, and must be treasured.

Let me pause a while, and drink a cup of some restorative before I resume.

FIVE

I have said it was a momentous night, and it was not done with me yet.

Spent, if not exhausted after my exertions, I lay wrapped about Ragnhild's body under the covers, barely credulous of my luck, and of the turnabout that had brought it. Outside the wind howled, but here were we in our warm lair, caring nothing for the world beyond. After a while we talked; I was eager to know whether I'd pleased her, for there was no doubting that she knew more about these matters than I did. But Ranghild's thoughts, it transpired, ran elsewhere. After kissing me and murmuring a few words, she came to the nub of things.

'You must know that this cannot happen again, Yorick.'

I swallowed, feeling a surge of disappointment.

'Enjoy me this one night, but I must be gone by daybreak. And it shall be a secret between us – as it is betwixt Dorethe and me. I ask you to swear to it.'

I hesitated: the rest of the troupe would have a fair notion of what I'd been up to, I thought. But she was ahead of me.

'As for your fellow players, if they know you must beg them not to speak of it. You see, I'm to be married soon.'

Confiteo: I was stunned. Like many a novice in matters of the heart, in my then blissful state I'd already allowed my mind to compass further trysts with this, my first lover; as yet I could imagine no other. Thoughts flew about my head, which I struggled to put into words.

'What if you found yourself... I mean to say, were you to become... that is-'

'If there is a child, it shall be mine,' Ragnhild said, cutting me short. 'It matters little who sired him, or her.'

'Do you mean that?' I asked. 'Would you keep truth hidden from your husband?'

'There's nothing to keep hidden,' was her reply. 'It could as well be his as yours – but you're seeing dangers where there are none. I asked you to swear – do you so?'

'I do,' I answered, mighty chastened; it was a blow to find myself of less importance than I'd thought. 'I swear not to reveal what we've done, but I'll not forget it. I'll cherish the memory, all my days.'

She breathed a sigh, which I took for one of content. Whereupon, my curiosity aroused, I asked who was the man she would marry, and did I know him?

'You do,' she answered. 'He's Trostann, the farrier's son.'

I must have given a start, for she raised her head. 'Does that trouble you?'

'It does a little,' I answered. But in truth, my first thought was not that I had cuckolded my old friend by rutting with his bride-to-be: rather, it was the notion that he'd not told me of his betrothal. Was I so sundered from him, now that I'd become a King's Player, as I was from my old stable fellows?

'Then you must master it,' Ragnhild was saying. Her face was close, her breath warm on my cheek. 'I have to make the best of whatever comes to me – as you've done, Yorick. Yet you'll have a good life, travelling and playing in fine places, while I'm bound to Kronborg. Think on that, before you judge me.'

'I do not judge,' I told her. 'What I feel is but regret, that we won't lie together like this again. And envy for Trostann... he's most fortunate.'

In the dark, I believe she smiled. 'He is,' she said pertly, 'as am I. And I wouldn't want you to think I gave myself to just anyone with a cock.' She paused, settling herself against my shoulder again. 'You're a rare one, my buck... most uncommon. I've heard it said you had favours from the hex, down at the Sund.'

I drew a breath. 'Favours? No - my mother took me as a child, to have her tell my fortune, nothing more.'

'And did she? Tell your fortune?'

'In her fashion,' I said, 'though I didn't understand all of it. But it's of no importance, for I put little faith in such. Nowadays I make my own luck,' I added, with bold conceit. 'I study hard, and I will indeed make the best of it.'

'You'd be wise to do so,' Ragnhild said, with a trace of coolness. 'The King won't live for ever, and he has no son to name as his successor. You'll not always enjoy his protection.'

'I know that,' I answered, somewhat distractedly; for in truth I felt a fresh stirring in my loins just then, that promised further business. Putting aside thoughts of Trostann, the King and everything else, I slid my hand down and began to stroke her in the place where, as she'd said a while ago, it mattered.

To my delight, she responded at once. 'Well then,' she murmured, somewhat drowsily. 'Let's seize the hour while we may. Tomorrow we go to our work, and in the days to come we'll pass each other with a greeting, and no more. I'll marry, and you'll reap the rewards of what I've shown you this night – for there are a dozen maids in Kronborg who'll readily lie with you. Did you know that?'

'Are there?' I blurted. 'I hadn't thought on it...' I frowned. 'What was that, about what you've shown me this night?'

She let out a sigh, that stopped short of a laugh. 'See now, player boy, do you think we didn't know you were but a colt, untried and unbroken? It was my place to relieve you of your innocence - and at risk of flattering you, my pleasure too. It would either be me or that beanpole Thura, the skinniest of us all. But the plump maid won over the thin one.'

By the gods, how dumbstruck was I to hear those words! Even my cock was chastened, and began to wilt at once. Was I merely a chart, I wondered, to be read by anyone with eyes in their head - even the spindle-thin Thura, considered the dullest girl in Kronborg? My thoughts whirling, I resolved to confront her at a later date, and see what might come of it.

Yes, *confiteo* again: I was on the way already to becoming a new Yorick. Yorick the Rake, who never failed to exercise his impatient cock whenever and with whomever chance allowed, and who won a reputation for spreading his seed about Helsingor and beyond. The Yorick who would one day pay the price for it...

Alas, I have strayed again. I beg pardon, for in truth there's someone who has been chafing to get on to this page, and who will wear me down soon enough. I ask her patience: she'll have her due reward, if not to the extent of outshining all others, as no doubt she would expect. Return with me to the brewing-house and to Ragnhild, her body warm against mine, her hand clutching my shrinking cock, her voice uncertain now in the gloom.

'What, Yorick? Have I dismayed you?'

'No...' I struggled to master myself. 'No... I've been a poor observer – more, I've been a dolt. I'm thankful it was you who cleaved to me and not Dorethe – let alone Thura the pikestaff. Let's do as you say, and enjoy the night... there,' I added with relief, feeling my wilful cock swelling anew. 'Try me again - nay, instruct me. For a fairer teacher no man had in all Denmark, sweet Ragnhild...'

At which her laughter burst forth, sending a drop of spittle straight into my eye.

'What a word-weaver you are!' she exclaimed. 'And yet for all your honey-tongued speech, as shameless as any I've known. Then again...' she paused, lowering her voice. 'It doesn't displease me. Now cease talking, and fall to – and remember.'

'I will,' I gulped. And I do.

And yet, the very next day after my sweat-slathered, thrusting, groaning night with Ragnhild, thoughts of her and almost everything else were driven from my mind - at least for a while, as were those of everyone in Kronborg and beyond. For that same night, while the King feasted his knights and nobles in the High Hall, and his players delighted the company with their skills, and Yorick played the lady's maid in his yellow hairpiece and padded smock, another event had occurred which was unknown to all but a very few until the morning. Away from the drinking and carousing, in her tapestried chamber in a bed hung with tasselled velvet, the Queen died of a seizure. And her last words, if her maidservants' accounts be true, were not ones of piety or devotion, but of rage and bitterness.

'So the royal stag shall outlive me!' She is said to have wailed, while her body shook like a reed in a gale. 'Shame upon him - let him fall into a lake of boiling ordure when his time comes, and his voice be lost to all eternity! I give thanks that I'll never hear it again, nor have sight of him! A pox and a plague on Rorik and on his progeny, whoever they are! Now, Lord of Heaven - let me quit this earth!'

But harken to this: a snowfall came later that day, shrouding the country with the purest, downy white. And though a mourning was declared, in truth there were few tears shed at the Queen's passing, nor did any pall of gloom settle over Rorik's kingdom. There was a chill silence, and an unspoken air of relief.

And Dorethe, the belle of the castle, remained chaste and unassailable until she caught the eye of a visiting nobleman who bore her away forever. They say a sigh was heard all over Kronborg... and that too, brought a kind of relief.

For Yorick and his fellows, it was a lean time that followed. For months there were no feasts, no raucous nights in the High Hall with drinking bouts and foolery, and no call for the players to perform. Only Makan was called to the King's side, to console him in his grief for the loss of his Queen, his chamberlain said. But most people knew better: that far from being grief-stricken Rorik was taking his ease, conferring with his trusted lords and counsellors, compassing the future. It was too soon to talk of his remarrying, or even of bringing some favoured lady into Kronborg to be chambered close to him; though in truth, few would have begrudged him that pleasure. Yet he did talk of the succession, and the hard choices that must be made - which brings me at last to speak of his only surviving child, the wilful Gurutha.

There: I have kept her back until now, but can delay no longer; and though I cover her name with reverence, the sentiment is bound up with fear and memories of treachery. Yet I've sworn to reveal all, which is why my fervent hope is not merely that I live to finish my tale, but that I will die before anyone reads it. *Confiteo*: Yorick, for all his fame and favours, his reputed wit, is a shameful coward. For were the truth known concerning his relations with the Princess – daughter of Rorik and his Queen and, so it's said, the bitter fruit of their last coupling together – he might well be dragged from his chamber and put to a terrible death.

It was the following spring when I first came to know the young Gurutha, who was by that time perhaps fourteen years of age, yet with the arrow-sharp mind of a grown woman. Until then she had been a mere presence at Kronborg, glimpsed so rarely and guarded so closely that it was believed she was sickly, even slow-witted. The Queen, it was well known, was cold towards her daughter, holding the poor infant to blame for her own arrival via the long agony of a terrible childbirth; an event which, it was also known, caused her mother to shun the King's presence in her bed thereafter, of which I have told already. Hence the child grew up with only her nurses for company, forbidden to sit in the High Hall and as time went by, barely spoken of and then with little more than pity. Yet now, with the death of her mother, a change was come: King Rorik commanded that henceforth the Princess would take her place at his side, and join him at times in riding out to survey his realm.

For the matter is, the King adored Gurutha and always had. She was just one cause of the rift between him and his Queen - but while the Queen held grudge against her daughter, Rorik did not. And though he allowed the Princess's seclusion to continue through her childhood years, he also made certain that she had the best of care, and that her tutors were drawn from among the most learned men in Denmark. One of these men later became tutor to Yorick too, to his disgust – his disgust, that is, not Yorick's; but I leap ahead again.

The Princess Gurutha, then, was a most singular maiden: pert and quick-witted, vain and self-willed, well-formed and pretty, most flirtatious for one of her years, and so fickle that she became somewhat terrifying. Woe betide the careless stableman who failed to have her pony saddled and ready when she chose to ride forth at a moment's notice, as she was now wont to do, with a guard of horsemen in attendance. Woe betide one of those same horsemen, should he ride too close to her - or by contrast, fall too far behind: judging the right distance from Gurutha was always a matter of delicacy. So was divining her will, which was as changeable as the wind on the Sund: this moment she demanded sweet wine and cakes, the next baked meats and claret, though the last was as rare at Kronborg as unicorns. And pity that handsome young serving-man who was unlucky enough to find himself the subject of Gurutha's attention one evening, when she chanced upon him in a passageway. Even though she was accompanied by a maid, and the young man would have no more thought of touching the Princess than he would of leaping into a whirlpool, the result was disaster: for his insolence in accepting her unexpected kiss on the lips, he was flogged and dismissed from royal service, to be replaced by a pock-marked fellow with a stoop. In truth, when it came to his daughter, King Rorik was a fool who doted on her and indulged her every whim, as if he were eager to atone for those years when his Queen kept her apart, driving him out to make war upon the unfortunate Norwegians.

All of this Yorick and his fellows knew and ruminated on as they sat in their quarters that springtime, idle and unwanted. Even Jofurr was bored, and had taken to curling himself in a corner with, so Niall claimed, a look of disgust. The company had practised new tricks, learned new songs and studied a new interlude Eghil had somehow got from England, letting it be known that we were eager to perform at the King's pleasure. But no such order came, and Eghil's mind turned in another direction: to beg the King's permission to leave the palace and go travelling, taking our shows to other parts of his kingdom. It would be a new experience for Yorick, he was told - and more, it would do him good to be away from the women hereabouts, with several of whom he was now shamelessly and notoriously intimate.

Yes, even Ragnhild was little more than a memory now, though she and I always exchanged courtesies when our paths crossed. She married Trostann early that spring, and they were content; I even caroused with him on his wedding-night, taking care not to drink too much and let something spill out. From Ragnhild I had moved on to the beanpole Thura, who proved to be a disappointment: I'll not set down details – nor has it any bearing on my skills, let me add. Women are of many kinds, I learned, and wiser from the garnering of such knowledge, I put Thura behind me and bedded the next one: Bodil, the flower of the brewing-house – scene of my first, unforgettable experience of carnality with Ragnhild – where she worked with her father the brew-master. And after Bodil the brewing maid came Hella and Hertha, who were sisters, followed by...

Well, *satis* – enough, you might say. But have I not promised to *call to mind the impurity of my life past*, as well as *the unclean corruptions of my soul*? Hence, I'll not deny what I did. Mattheus the scholar-chaplain would likely be praying for my soul if he saw what I write: that when all's said and sifted, Yorick is a coward, a swaggerer and a lecher. But one thing he is not, is too stupid for his own good.

There came a most memorable day when I walked out in spring sunshine, restless and bored with listening to the players' gossip. Presently I wandered into the King's garden, where Makan and I used to pick fallen fruit, and where the cherry trees were in flower. Walking slowly, head down in careless thought, I was unaware that there were others nearby until a voice called out. Looking round, I saw two figures gazing in my direction: one was a maid named Runa, and the other was her mistress, the Princess Gurutha. Abashed, I dropped to one knee, half-expecting some rebuke for being there. My unease grew when the Princess came towards me, stepping lightly in her shoes of fine red leather.

'You're the jester's boy.'

I risked an upward glance and saw her looking down on me with a half-smile, which I took for one of mockery. 'Indeed, Highness... I'm Yorick.'

'I've heard a good deal about you, Master Yorick,' Gurutha announced with some severity. Was I about to earn a comeuppance for some recent exploit, I wondered? Stuck for a reply, I lowered my head.

'Leave us,' she said. I looked up again, about to rise, then realised that the words had been addressed to Runa.

'My Lady?' Runa had no liking for the order; no doubt her instructions were to remain at the Princess's side at all times. Stuck between obedience to the King's will and that of his wayward daughter, she hesitated – which brought a swift response.

'I said go – at once!'

The maid and I both flinched: it was nothing less than a shriek, which chilled me to the bone. In a trice Runa turned and hurried away, gathering her skirts as she went. Yorick still knelt, wishing he were somewhere else.

'Stand up,' came the next, snapped command.

I stood up, staring down at my shoes.

'I know you're clever and have a talent for entertaining, like Makan,' Gurutha said. 'Who's even now sitting with my father, sharing wine and discourse – men's talk that is kept from me as if I were a child, too foolish to understand.'

She fell silent. The silence grew longer, until I made myself look up, whereupon:

'Do you think a queen should have her own jester, Yorick?'

'I see no reason why she should not, Highness... if she wishes,' I answered, hoping that was what she wanted to hear.

'And what of a princess? Should she too not enjoy such a privilege?'

In dismay at the direction she appeared to be taking, I gulped. 'Again, I cannot see why she should not, if-'

I was cut short by her sudden laugh: girlish and giggly, for all her pretended worldliness. In some embarrassment, I waited.

'For pity's sake, be at ease,' she said. 'I've no intention of taking you as my fool... there are enough fools about Kronborg already.' And when I looked puzzled, she grew alarmingly coquettish. 'As it happens, I might have quite a different task in mind for you.'

Dumbstruck, I met her eye, in fear and in hope that her meaning was other than what I thought – such conceit had Yorick! As if Rorik's daughter would stoop to relations with a stable-boy-turned-player, the whelp of Gitte the Three-fingered. So accustomed was he to getting his own way with those he pursued – more often than not, at least – that he saw any creature in skirts as a potential conquest. But Gurutha was a child, whatever she thought of herself, and one of royal blood. Such thoughts swirled about in my muddled head until I was brought to earth with a thud.

'You'll not be my jester,' the Princess said. 'But you could be my eyes and ears at Court. Sit close to my father along with Makan, seeming to learn his ways while listening to all that's said between the King and his counsellors – especially when it concerns me. Do you follow?'

'I confess I do not, Highness,' I said, while a cold hand seemed to clutch my heart. 'If you speak of–'

'I think you understand perfectly what I speak of, Yorick,' came the retort. 'Think: I shall be a queen one day, and besides, old Makan won't live much longer - have you heard how he wheezes? You could rise, sooner than you might think and higher than you've ever dreamed – or are you too slow-witted to see it?'

'I don't believe so, my lady,' I muttered. I was stung, yet kept to my part as the contrite servant. 'But in any case, the players are likely to be gone soon for the summer, if the King will allow it. Hence–'

'He won't,' Gurutha said at once. 'I'll ask that they remain here instead, and he will honour my wish.'

I fell silent, whereupon she assumed another of those knowing half-smiles of hers: *gammelklog* she was called by the servants – precocious. Assuming a gentler tone, she went on: 'You can be a *hofnar* like Makan – his apprentice, if you like - but you will also be my spy. It can be our secret. So, are you willing? If not, I'll take it as an affront – I expect you know what that would mean.'

She extended a pale hand, her slender fingers bright with rings, and kept it there until I knelt to kiss it. Then she turned it, palm open, by which I understood that I should take it and rise to my feet.

As I did so, the sun clouded over - but one thing remained clear enough: I would in all likelihood become Gurutha's creature, and henceforth must submit to her will.

That, too, still causes me to shudder.

SIX

It was a summer of great heat, when crops withered in the fields and streams began to run dry. The people of Kronborg sweltered, the stables stank insufferably, and Yorick was in a turmoil such as he'd never known.

My first thought after my encounter with the Princess was to go to Makan and tell him of it - surely he would know what to do? Whereupon a memory of Gurutha's face, her greedy little eyes and sly smile, would spring up to fill me with doubt. Makan, I believed, would be sorely troubled; his loyalty to the King was bottomless and unquenchable, yet his concern for me would tear him. And so I delayed, pondering my course of action miserably, which my fellow players soon noticed. Eghil believed the cause was merely a restlessness to be gone for the summer travelling, which all of them were eager to undertake – until, to their dismay, the order came from the King refusing them leave to depart. His players were forbidden to go further afield than Helsingor, he announced, and should instead be ready to entertain at the royal will. Which in my private gloom, I understood, meant the will of the fearsome Gurutha. Hence, when the others gathered to decide how best to deal with the matter, Yorick fled from the castle and took himself down to the Sund, driven by a sudden desire to see the hex Edela.

I cannot recall what drove me to seek her out; perhaps I barely knew. In those days I seldom thought of the woman, who was grown old and frail, it was said, and less willing to help those who sought her advice. Though I'd never forgotten the night Gitte had taken me to Edela's hut, the memory was dulled. Once the notion arrived in my head, however, I knew it might offer, if not a solution to my quandary, then at least a wise and untrammelled ear to hear of it. Hence on a hot afternoon, with the Sund stretching away into a haze, I made my way down to the shore and strode northwards, past the last fisherman's house and along the rocky strand, the distance somehow greater than I remembered it. There was no wind, the low hills above shimmering in the heat as I peered ahead, seeking the hex's tumbledown dwelling. When at last I came upon it, it appeared smaller than I recalled. Wedged into a slope, as if part of the earth itself, it was little more than a hovel of poles and branches, sagging with old turves. But there was the pen with a single goat in it, regarding me over the rickety fence, and a few hens strutting about, and the rough-hewn door open towards the sea as before. I halted outside, uncertain now of the kind of welcome I might receive. There was no smoke from the roof, nor any other sign of life apart from the animals. Yet I knew she was there, as I knew she was aware of my arrival. I stayed, until at last the stooped figure of the hex appeared in the doorway, shielding her eyes from the sunlight.

'Erik,' she murmured, taking a slow step forward; she walked with a stick of hazel, her brown hand gripping its knobbed head fiercely.

'I ask pardon for not visiting you for so long,' I blurted; those black eyes, that I now remembered as if but a day had passed since I was there, were as searching as ever. And I was a child again, standing by his mother's skirts, wondering what would become of him. I could picture Gitte standing in the fading light, calm and still as she spoke to the hex.

'I heard you were with your mother when she died,' Edela said.

'I was.'

'Did she tell you things?'

'About herself,' I answered. I was eager to question her, but she stayed me.

'The Queen always wished to be rid of her. She thought Gitte was accursed, and brought ill luck to Kronborg... and yet, what's past is past.' She looked away for a while, towards the Sund, then: 'There's bad blood in the house of Rorik Slyngebond, boy. Old banes, that will one day come to fruition.'

I lowered my gaze: far from finding comfort, I found, I was being given more grim news to add to my troubles.

'Yet your good fortune holds,' Edela said, as if to counter my thoughts. 'You've thrived... a man now, if one of questionable character.'

It was true enough, and I was shamed: her eyes seemed to burn into mine. While I searched for some reply, she went on:

'Now you're at a fork in the road, and uncertain which one to take.'

I nodded to her, with a stirring of hope. If anyone could see a way out of this mire I was in, I thought, it should be Edela. 'It was not of my choosing,' I told her. 'It's as though I've been set adrift on a dangerous sea - and I cannot swim.'

The hex made no answer.

'My father... Makan, I mean... is ageing, and I wish to aid him. Yet another would use me, for her instrument,' I blundered on. 'I had hopes you might point me the right way...'

'It's not my custom to tell a grown man what he should do,' Edela said. 'You must decide for yourself.'

'When I came here as a child,' I countered, 'you asked me what I would be. And I-'

'You gave your answer,' the hex said, cutting me short. 'It's your calling, is it not? To be at the whim of highborn folk. Though less a stallion than a performing dog, dancing obeisance.'

I drew breath: did she scorn me now? 'And yet,' I said, 'my choice remains: do as I'm bid and play two roles at once, betraying not only my beloved father, but even the King we both serve. Or refuse and face the consequences – which could be terrible.'

'There's another,' Edela said. 'You could run away, and seek a life elsewhere.'

I gazed at her: was this some sort of challenge, as I vaguely remembered she had set me before? I could tell nothing from her tone. I remained silent, hoping she would say more, but instead she gave an impatient shrug.

'Weigh your choices, Erik,' she said, somewhat tiredly. 'And cut your own path. May good fortune ever go with you - I don't believe we'll see each other again.'

'Wait,' I said, with some urgency. 'Will you not tell me what you saw, that night I sat at your table? Were there things writ in my palm, that you wouldn't tell me?'

She paused, looked at the ground, then lifted her eyes.

'I believe the notion came to me, that the one who buries you will also dig you up,' was her reply. 'Other than that, I forget.'

And she was gone, shuffling into the hut, her fingers knotted about the hazel-stick.

I left her, more disheartened and less enlightened than when I'd arrived.

Yet by the time I returned to the castle I had formed my resolve, though it troubled me. I had no desire to leave Kronborg, and everyone I knew. Instead I would seek out Makan and tell him the Princess Gurutha wanted me to come to the Court and learn his skills. If he was willing, and if the King would allow it, I would then go to Eghil and tell him I must leave his company. That, at least, would do some good: when I told the Princess I would serve her as she wished, I could also beg her to ask the King to release the players from his service. Once free of Yorick, my friends could travel all summer if they wished, and prosper by it. I saw no reason why she should refuse that request.

If only it had been so simple.

I accosted Makan that same night, coming from the High Hall where the King was dining with a few of his closest friends - and received a shock. I hadn't seen him for a week, perhaps longer, and his appearance alarmed me: seldom had I known him look so weary and careworn. Instead of going up to his chamber I urged him to come with me to the kitchens, where I begged a bowl of hot broth from spindly Thura. She served us with a poor grace, taking the opportunity to remind me of her low opinion of Cock-master Yorick, though Makan failed to notice. He sat hunched at the old table in the corner where we had often eaten when I was a child, and Gitte was alive, and tow-haired Erik was popular with the kitchen folk. I asked if he wanted some wine, being prepared to wrangle with the hatchet-faced Thura if need be, but he shook his head.

'The King would have me drunk most nights, if I let him,' he murmured, with a tired smile. 'As if I could banter with him, with a head dulled by wine. I pretend to take a sip from my cup, and spill some of it in clowning, then sip some more until I've diverted him.' He spooned broth into his mouth, then said: 'I'd thought he would be easier in himself, after the Queen died. Yet he drinks harder than ever... I believe it's on account of the Princess.'

He was looking across the table at me, and on a sudden my designs crumbled to dust; I could no more have kept a truth from Makan than I could outmatch him in jesting. When I met his eye, he went on: 'She plays him like a pipe, Erik – a wise old warrior like Rorik – just as she does everyone else. It was her wish that the players be forbidden to leave Kronborg... then, I expect you know it.'

I nodded, trying to put my thoughts in order. 'She'll not be gainsaid,' I ventured. 'I pity her servants, who must bend in all directions at once.'

'Or lose their place,' Makan went on. 'Even a Favoured Fool... if she demanded my dismissal from the Court, I fear the King might agree to it.'

I was astounded. 'But you're the one who lifts his humour when no other can. He tells you things he tells no-one else – that's what Gitte always said.'

'He did,' Makan allowed. 'But age changes a man, Erik. Now he falls into maudlin talk about having no sons, and being too old to sire any. Though in truth...' he paused, put on a leery smile and looked about the kitchen in the manner of a stage conspirator, which caused me to laugh: he had not lost his touch. 'There are both boys and girls elsewhere about the Kingdom who bear an odd resemblance to King Rorik - have you heard?'

'I have – and of women whose husbands are the richer for it. So, could he not name one of their offspring as his heir, if he wished to?'

'He could,' Makan replied. 'Yet he's set on the Princess becoming Queen, and will find a husband for her. Likely one who'll indulge her every whim... don't you pity the poor fellow?'

'I do,' I said – and decided to speak of my predicament. I should have done so from the start; indecision was but one of Yorick's failings, back then.

'There's something I must tell you,' I said with a glance towards Thura, who was at the other side of the room. 'It concerns the same matter... of the Princess Gurutha's future, I mean.'

Makan regarded me, then put down his spoon and spoke low. 'Ah... she's asked you too, has she? To be her eyes and ears in the King's presence?'

I drew breath, but had no answer; as always, he was ahead of me.

'She came to me, months ago,' he went on. 'The little vixen. I refused to tell tales and betray my King – told her I'd sooner die. More, if she threatened me, I said I'd tell him all. She's yet a child... thinks she can have her own way in everything.'

I gave a nod, and Makan threw me a smile. 'So, having been rebuffed by her father's old jester, Gurutha went to his boy.' He thought for a moment, then: 'Which is why she asked the King that his players be forbidden to leave – so that you too would remain. Do I understand, then, that you refused her?'

'Not quite,' I answered, with a mixture of shame and relief. 'In truth, I've not given her an answer. I've kept out of her sight - hiding in corners as if I were a spy already, while Eghil and the others are stuck in Kronborg. But I intend to remedy it if I can... that is, I thought it would be the better course. To submit to her wishes, I mean - I can see no other way.'

'Can you not?' Makan wore a crafty look. 'Have you forgotten what I taught you, about-?'

'Doing the unexpected? No, I don't forget. But what other course is there?'

'There is one which might profit us both,' was his reply. 'That you and I work together – in the King's interests as well as our own. What do you say to that?'

He picked up his spoon and resumed eating, allowing me to ponder the matter - which I did most eagerly. What Gurutha expected, of course, was that I would bow to her request. And it appeared she hadn't guessed that Makan would tell me of her approach to him – a misjudgement on her part. Perhaps, I reasoned, the sly princess was not so clever as she believed – and hence the notion that Makan and I could conspire together might never occur to her. Yet, I wondered, how would this work? Would I have to lie to her, or…?

'Turn it about,' Makan said, breaking my thoughts. 'Think how we might keep the King's confidence, yet satisfy young Gurutha's desire for news. Which desire, you will understand, is only for tidings concerning herself – not least the plans her father has to find her a husband. She cares nothing for the kingdom, for the greater matters of war and state. So we may bore her with tedious reportage of land and laws, say, or of conflict with Norway, or other stuff - even if we must concoct them between us.'

'We would tread on dangerous ground,' I objected. 'Should she learn from her father that we've been untruthful, or spun tales out of thin air…'

'Then I would go to the King and tell him all,' Makan interrupted. 'Or at least, threaten to do so. Rorik would be dismayed to think she cared so little for him – that his love has blinded him to her faults. Would she truly risk his displeasure, I would say to her, when he has the power to marry her off to anyone he likes?'

With a smile tugging at my mouth, I shook my head; no-one else could ease my heart as Makan did. I cover his name with love and admiration – as I wish he were alive to divert me with his rhymes and jests. I see him now, waving his spoon about as he laid out his plan, while Thura scowled at us from a corner. On impulse, I beckoned to her to come over.

'A *penning* for you, Thura, if you'll bring us each a cup of Rhenish,' I said boldly. 'A jester's work is thirsty work… will you not have one drink?' I asked Makan.

'Well, I will,' he answered with a look at Thura, who went grudgingly off to comply. To me, he said: 'Are you willing then, to aid me when I entertain my master? To leave the player's life, for one of constant abasement and derision?'

My smile faded at those words; in truth, I realised then, I had hardly ever seen Makan at work amusing the King and his Court, not being present at such times except when I'd played the servant to Sveinn's lustful lady. I knew that Makan was often wearied by his efforts, and had at times been morose while Gitte was alive, yet I knew little of what went on in the King's privy company. And yet, there was no doubt in my mind that this was the path to take. Had not Edela herself said it was my calling – even though it be that of a performing dog?

'I'll always be proud to study and learn from you,' was my answer. 'It's what Gitte wanted too - though I fear I lack your wit.'

'It's not me you should study, Erik,' Makan replied. 'It's the King. Observe his moods, his fancies - what pleases him and what irks him. Your brief time as a player will not be wasted, and you have a bent for mockery. Imitate the voices of those about you, for Rorik likes mimicry. If Sveinn will teach you some songs, all the better. This is your schooling, though you be a man already. So, will you be steadfast? For there's no turning aside, once you and I are set on this.'

He was most serious now, his moist old eyes peering into mine. For answer, I reached out and gripped his hand. And when Thura came with the cups of good Rhineland wine we drank in silence, eyes locked above the brims, close in our new understanding.

That night Yorick slept like a dead man, the strain of recent weeks leaving him at last, and awoke afresh to greet the new day – *ecce aurora*! By mid-morning he had sought audience with the Princess Gurutha and sworn to be her messenger, reporting on what passed between the King and others in secret. And if her response was only a languid show of approval, together with a rebuke for my tardiness in bringing the answer she expected, it troubled me not a whit. For it struck me then, as it had before, that the girl was but a player herself – and one whose skills compared poorly with those of Eghil and his company. Which company I returned to later in the day, having made my request of Gurutha on their behalf. I went to express my regret at having to leave them – but was confounded to receive the response I did.

They sat about the room, all four of them eying me warily. Niall had Jofurr curled up on his lap, Sveinn and Freybjorn sat together conning some piece of play-text. Even Eghil looked coolly upon me. That they knew what I was about to say seemed clear: little escaped those sharp-eyed fellows. So, thinking I'd best get it done, I cleared my throat and began – to be cut short almost at once.

'I'm told we have you to thank, for bringing about the King's leave to depart from Kronborg after all,' Eghil said. 'Word came to me at mid-day... Her Highness the Princess, it seems, begged her father to change his mind. What changed the Princess's mind, however, is another question. For it was she who had us moored here, like a ship that's quarantined. Is that not so?'

I gulped; secrecy, I thought ruefully, was a scarce commodity hereabouts. How much did he and the others know? Yet this was no time for dissembling: I adored these men who, aside from Trostann, were as the brothers I never had. Seeing all their eyes upon me, I gave a nod.

'It is so,' I said. 'You know she can't be refused, whatever she wishes.'

'And why did she wish it, Yorick?' Sveinn asked, eyebrows raised as high as only he could manage. 'She never showed such interest in her father's players before... most curious, wouldn't you say?'

I was caught, and they knew it. With sinking spirits, I sought for some words of contrition until Niall spoke up and confounded me.

'If the gossips speak truly, it appears the headstrong Gurutha has set her sights on sprightly Yorick,' he said. 'For a plaything – or even more. She's been seen alone with him, talking most privately... perhaps she wished to keep him close, and so had the King keep all his players on a leash.'

Stuck for an answer I looked at Eghil, who now appeared more hurt than angry.

'What saddens me, Yorick, is why you didn't confide in us,' he said. 'We might have arrived at some solution... or do you doubt that?'

'I do not,' I said, 'and you shame me. More,' I added, 'I should have offered to quit the company at once, so that without me you would have been free to travel.'

'Instead you skulked in nooks and corners,' Freybjorn said. 'Now you've come - yet somewhat late, is it not?'

He addressed this to Eghil, who eyed me and said: 'I'd already made my decision, Yorick. I was resolved to beg the King to dismiss you from the troupe, and give us leave to travel without you.'

Well, *confiteo*: despite my relief, I was hurt. 'Was I such a trial to you?' I asked. 'An appendage, without skills to contribute, taken on as a favour to Makan, who would in turn speak well of you to the King? Perhaps you never wanted me from the beginning...'

'Cease your whining, Yorick,' Sveinn broke in. 'You would have made a fine player, and you know it well enough. You're probably as born a dissembler as any I've known, though we all believe you're a clown and not a tragedian. Doubtless you'll prosper, sitting at the King's footstool – that's where your future lies, is it not?'

After a moment, I nodded; there seemed little more to say. I was about to take my leave, but Eghil stayed me.

'We're leaving Kronborg tomorrow,' he said. 'And if you'll swear to guard this confidence, it will be our lasting farewell. We mean to shake the dust of Rorik's kingdom from our feet and take our chances elsewhere... Mecklenburg perhaps, or Anhalt, or the Low Countries.' He sighed, then: 'There are ghosts hereabouts, and I don't intend to become one of them. I've a son in Bremen I've not seen since he was an infant; mayhap he'll follow my calling, and return here to play before some other king... one who's less in thrall to his offspring.'

'I swear I'll keep your confidence,' I answered, my heart heavy on a sudden. 'And if you're truly resolved not to come back, we will all be the poorer for it – Yorick more than anyone, mere clown that he is.'

I looked round at them, most sadly, and saw that their coolness had melted away. As one they rose and came to me: Niall with Jofurr wrapped around one arm, Sveinn with a look of sadness, even Freybjorn wearing a smile. They embraced me in turn, Eghil last of all.

'Remember, Yorick,' he said, 'there will always be a place for you with us, should you wish. Wherever we are, find us and rejoin the company of fools, in which I baptised you.'

Whereupon, with a heavy heart, I left them to make their preparations.

I believe now that they were the last true friends I had, apart from the beloved boy. And, Sveinn never did teach me any of his songs.

SEVEN

One week later, on a still day of summer, Yorick was brought before Rorik Slyngebond, King of all Denmark, by his fool Makan, and made the lowest bow he could before that great carved throne. Never had I been so close to the monarch, yet alone looked him in the face as I did then - not even when, as a stable-lad, I had saddled his horse and watched him ride off to hawking or hunting. Back then I stood aside with others, averting my gaze; now I was forced to meet those sea-grey eyes above the brown beard which covered most of his cheeks. And the first thing he said to me was:

'So: you're Gitte's child, who wasn't supposed to see the dawn.'

'I am, Highness,' I answered – and was chilled by the thought that sprang up. It was a memory of the dying Gitte telling me this man could be my father – something I'd never spoken of to anyone, not even Makan. Those years of pushing the notion aside as some fancy of my mother's fell away in a trice, so that I swallowed loud enough to be heard.

'What - is this modesty, or fear?' the King asked, turning to Makan.

'I told him to wear brown breeches,' Makan said. 'Just to be safe.'

'Yet he wishes to be my fool, and take your place when you finally drop,' came the royal reply. 'Have you time enough left to teach him?'

'I thought it likely I wouldn't need it,' Makan said. 'Seeing as you're so unsteady on your legs these days. I wonder you don't have a little cart made, so you can be wheeled about.'

'He's the one would wheel me, being young and strong,' the King retorted. 'Does he carry you up to bed at night? And, can he drink?'

This last question was thrown at Yorick, who was abashed. What had I expected from Makan – a cringing fealty to his master? How little I knew about the nature of their friendship, or the degree of license Rorik's jester had to insult him. Then, no other could have carried it with the skill my almost-father had, drawing laughter where another would have brought disaster on his head. I forced a smile, and assure the King that I could down a mug or two, and match any man.

'That's bold,' Rorik said. 'Not to say rash... I've no patience with a fellow who makes claims he can't fulfil.'

'I'll learn with all due diligence, Highness,' I said, thinking fast. 'Drinking shall be a part of my studies, along with rhyming, and... mimicking,' I added hastily, recalling my talk with Makan in the kitchen – and at once regretted it.

'Who can you mimic?' Rorik demanded, frowning upon me. 'Show us.'

Now I was dumbstruck; even Makan, I knew, was unable to help me. Casting about desperately for someone whose speech I could reproduce at such short notice, and finding no-one, I was on the point of making an excuse when one person, and one person only, came to mind: she who had been most in my thoughts for weeks. Without thinking of the consequences – being accused of treason merely one of them – I put on a coy expression, fluttered my eyelids and spoke in the high voice of the Princess Gurutha.

'Why, how cross you look, dearest father!' I trilled. 'The poor young man is clearly terrified... have mercy, and let him try to please you in his way. My maid Runa thinks he shows promise, and who am I to dismiss her opinion?'

I broke off, coughed and drew breath; beside me I sensed Makan was taut. The silence that fell was profound - and one in which I believed my very life was held in the balance. Lowering my gaze, I stared at the floor of the presence chamber and awaited my fate. The silence seemed to last for an hour, until there came... what was it? A kind of rumble like cartwheels going past, or a roll of distant thunder - until realisation dawned, and I almost gasped with relief.

'By the gods, that's her!' Rorik shouted, with a roar of laughter that would have cracked a cauldron. 'The very echo of our daughter - whom you should thank for her absence! Had she heard, I dare not think what her response would have been... "who am I to dismiss her opinion"? Likely she'd demand your head on a block for your insolence, and we'd have been hard pressed to refuse her – it was bold, Yorick!'

See now, I don't exaggerate when I say that I sagged at the knees and might have dropped, had Makan not stuck out a steadying hand to grasp my shoulder – whereupon instead of praising me, he cuffed me roundly on the head.

'Forgive him, sire,' he muttered. 'There's fooling and there's foolishness, and he's yet to learn the difference betwixt the two. I never would have advised such effrontery, as you know. Have I leave to duck him in a horse-trough, or will you pronounce some fitter punishment?'

And yet, they were both smiling: two old men trading looks of understanding, borne of years spent in each other's company. They were more than master and servant - they were friends, if a king and a lowborn serf can ever be such. Putting on a scared look, I pretended to bite my nails in terror.

'Enough!' His smile fading, the King waved a dismissive hand. 'You've shown some skill, I'll allow, and I may call on you when fancy takes me… but first I have a question. What's the nature of your relations with the woman down at the Sund? I speak of the hex – that old scion of Hecate.'

I hesitated. My last visit to Edela had been observed, I realised, especially as it was made in broad daylight. Both Makan's and Rorik's eyes were upon me, as I tried to give the best answer I could. 'I believed myself at a fork in the road, Highness,' I said. 'I hoped she might tell my future, as she's done for others. There's no more to it than that, I swear.'

'And what was it she told you?'

'Only that I should trust my instincts, which were – which are – to study Makan and become the best fool I can, to the best King there has ever been…'

I stopped, cursing myself for falling to such flattery. Some monarchs, it's true, are susceptible to it, being blinded by their own conceit, but Rorik was not one of them. I saw the royal brow crease and struggled to form some better response, but it was too late.

'What sheep-shit,' the King said, in a tone of disappointment. 'I'll have none of it – I thought you'd have taught him that, at least,' he added, with a glance at Makan.

'The matter is, I've been too busy playing nursemaid to you,' Makan said sadly. 'Like seeing you don't drink too much, and wet your breeches.'

'It's my enemies who soil themselves, not me,' Rorik threw back. 'Like the English, once we got them by the balls - and none of your tired old jests about Danegeld,' he added, to which Makan smiled. Whereupon the King looked at me, and said: 'You're of no use in my court unless you speak the truth at all times - no matter how harsh you think it.'

'Indeed, I... I was instructed so, Highness,' I blathered. 'It was but my eagerness to please. My mother had hopes that I would follow Makan... if I fail at this as I failed as a player, then I'm nothing.'

A moment followed, in which I hoped he couldn't hear my heart galloping. Makan was calm, though he did not look at me. At last Rorik gave a grunt and appeared contented – until his next words sent me aflutter again.

'I've heard more about you, Yorick,' he said. 'You're a rutting stag among the servant girls, it seems – you've even caught the attention of the Princess Gurutha, whom you mimicked so well. While she in turn seems quite taken with you - how do you propose to deal with that?'

'Deal with it, Highness?' I blurted, with a sudden chill in my stomach. 'I swear I've not thought on it. I believe the Princess sees me as just another fool... a prentice to Makan, who might amuse her and her friends, being closer in age to them. She asked me if I thought a princess should have her own jester, and I told her I saw no reason why she shouldn't... was that wrong?'

Another of those silences followed, which would have troubled Yorick had not the blessed Makan come to his rescue. He gave a snort of disgust, and threw me a wry look.

'The conceit of youth,' he sighed. 'He means to show me up for an antic fool, whose ways are those of a bygone age. Then, there's no denying our days grow short...yours and mine,' he added, meeting the King's eye. 'So that, when comes the day that Queen Gurutha sits in your place along with her husband, who will keep the fires of laughter alive if not Makan's boy? For you and I will surely be a worms' banquet by then - indeed, in truth I...'

He broke off in dramatic fashion, startling the King and me as he clutched at his chest. With a little cry of pain he staggered, so that even Rorik half-rose in alarm, while Yorick's heart jumped - only for us both to gasp with relief, as a sly grin broke out on Makan's face.

'Your pardon,' he said, straightening himself up. 'It seemed as though I felt a twinge... one can never be certain, can one?' He raised an eyebrow at his master, who let out a great breath.

'You wicked old cunt!' The King exclaimed. 'I'll admit you had me then - as you had him too...' this with a nod in my direction. 'No more tricks like that, I say. Moreover, I insist on going to my tomb before you, do you hear? I order you to outlive me - on pain of death!'

Upon which, partly with relief and partly in delight at his own jest, he gave one of his great laughs which filled the room, and with which Makan and I could only join in. It was unfeigned on my part: at the release of such tautness I bent double and guffawed as if I were a boy again – as Trostann and I had done, in our happy days of play. What a tableau was there: the mighty Rorik, his Favoured Fool and Yorick the onetime stable-lad, helpless with laughter in the royal presence, and doubtless overheard far beyond it. Presently we grew calmer, laughs giving way to sniggers as we all three wiped our eyes. The King cleared his throat loudly and called for an attendant, who came running.

'Give this boy ten *pennings* as he leaves,' he ordered, 'and convey a request to the Princess Gurutha to attend us.' Then, turning to me: 'Go, take the rest of the day at your leisure. But - one last thing.'

He paused, long enough for me to feel uneasy; then came the warning.

'My daughter's affections are not to be taken lightly, Yorick,' the King said. 'You will never be alone with her again, nor do anything other than obey her to the very limit of your powers. For if I ever hear a rumour that you and she spoke intimately together - no matter what the cause – the consequences will be worse than your darkest thoughts could compass. Do you understand me?'

Whereupon with due humility, but chiefly in cold fear, Yorick assured his royal master not only that he understood, but that he would henceforth obey both him and the Princess without question to the very end of his days, strike him dead if every word wasn't true. And after making his bow, he was dismissed.

Well now, what a year that was which followed, though one that I struggle to recall clearly. By the following summer, with Eghil and the players long gone from Kronborg and sorely missed, Yorick was at pains to become the jester the King wished him to be, to the neglect of all else. Apart, that is, from his continuing cock-work with a number of pliant maids – not least those who were impressed by his new standing as second fool to Makan. And apart, of course, from his secret role as spy for the Princess Gurutha, the only shadow upon an otherwise promising life of service.

My spying for Gurutha began innocently enough, one of my earliest reports being word of the fine Friesland mare her father intended to present her with as a gift, the King having told Makan who then told me. And yet, far from delighting the Princess, the news was poorly received: she delighted in surprises, I discovered, and I had just ruined this one. I heard this not from Gurutha's own lips but from those of her maid, the modest and discreet Runa. For, after what the King had said, there was no possibility of Yorick finding himself alone with Gurutha again - which fortunately for him, the Princess had anticipated. Henceforth, she announced in a brief, neatly-written missive which I was to burn as soon as I'd read, her servant would be the one to whom I would make report – infrequently, and by word of mouth only. This was a relief since, as I told Runa, I could not read a word, hence she'd been obliged to spell her mistress's message out to me. So came the day, after news of the forthcoming gift-horse had been passed and the unfavourable reply received, when the maid and I faced each other in silence.

'How do you bear it?' I asked her at last. 'Having to attend Her Highness by the hour, never knowing whether your next words will please or enrage her?'

She gave a little shrug. She was very pretty, was Runa; slight and small-breasted, with a most alluring neck, from what I saw of it. In truth she was one of the few servants Yorick had never attempted to bed: to do so would have been foolhardy indeed, in view of whom she served. Finally, she gave a quick smile and said:

'I might ask the same question of you, Yorick. The worst I might receive for displeasing the Princess is a slap, or a switch across my back – whereas you...' she met my eye. 'Well, we're obliged to trust each other, are we not?'

'Indeed - and I do trust you,' I answered. 'There are others who would relish the chance to see me caught out and dealt the harshest of penalties. For them, it would be no more than I deserve.'

She looked quite sad to hear that. We were outside, in the King's garden where my first fateful encounter with Gurutha had taken place. She had ordered that my exchanges with Runa should always occur outdoors, with great care taken not to be overheard. Moreover, should we be observed as we were bound to be, rumour of a flirtation between us should not be denied: Yorick's reputation was such that any other explanation would be disbelieved. Though it was made clear to me from the outset by Gurutha, that should I lay but one fingertip upon her maid the consequences would be too dreadful to contemplate.

'One thing surprises me,' Runa said then. 'Since you're only rarely allowed to attend the King, how can you overhear his pronouncements? My guess is that Makan tells you what to say, is that so?'

I tautened; I should have foreseen that both Gurutha and her maid might reach such a conclusion. For despite Makan's efforts to have me included, it was true that King Rorik seldom called me to entertain him, which made me scour my brains to discover how to please him. In truth, I hadn't yet gained Makan's facility with words. Nor could I break the confidence between him and I, hence:

'My father would never betray his master's secrets,' I told her. 'Please don't speak of it again. He's dear to me - and aside from you, the only one I trust.'

'Very well, if that's what you wish.' Runa levelled a gaze at me, and I was shamed; this maiden deserved a better mistress, I thought, and better work than had been her lot since she was sixteen years old. Which, I'd learned by then, would be Gurutha's age on her next birthday, and not fifteen as I'd surmised. She was already marriageable, of course - a fact that was lost on nobody, especially her father. Sooner or later there would be talk of her betrothal, and Yorick should be within royal earshot to learn of it. As I took my leave of Runa that day, I resolved to find a way to be at the King's side more often; somehow, Makan and I must contrive it between us.

And yet, by the end of that summer other matters had diverted me. For one thing, Makan grew weaker and frailer, so that it was no longer a jest that I sometimes had to help him up to the old chamber of a night-time, the room I now shared with him as I'd done as a boy. And for another: word came from the folk down at the Sund that the hex Edela had died in her sleep, stretched out as if ready for burial with her hair unbound and combed out, hands folded across her chest.

Within hours of the discovery, her goat ran away and her old hut blew down in a gale, becoming but a tangled mass of branches and turves that, quite soon, could no longer be distinguished from the hillside where it had stood.

She was the last hex any of us knew, and now there was no-one to tell the future.

EIGHT

It was in the hard midwinter, with Yuletide lately past, that Yorick at last found a way to make himself companionable to the King. He arrived at this happier state with the aid of two tutors: one, of course, his almost-father Makan; the other, to his surprise, the Princess's maid, Runa. Runa, it turned out, was possessed not only of a fine singing voice but also of a goodly store of songs learned at her mother's knee, which it was her custom to sing to her mistress at night-time. On learning of which, Yorick lost no time in demanding that she teach him.

'I wanted Sveinn the player to instruct me,' I told her, the two of us standing in the cold with only the brewing-house wall for shelter from the wind. 'He never found the time, but cannot you? Have you a bawdy rhyme or two, that might make the King chuckle?'

'I have not,' Runa replied, somewhat primly. 'I know only songs of romance, such as the Frankish troubadours make. You'd best look elsewhere.'

'I'll pay you,' I said, but to no avail; she could teach me some tunes, she allowed, but had no words suited to the kind of raucous feasts Rorik had been wont to hold – and which he was starting to hold again, the mourning period for the late Queen being past. Indeed, there was a banquet set for a fortnight hence, when the King's old friend Gerwendil, Lord of Jutland, was to be favoured guest. Makan and I had been preparing some clownage for the occasion, but a few songs wouldn't go amiss, I reasoned. I was about to press Runa further, but she was shivering and eager to go inside, until a thought occurred.

'Why don't you fashion your own rhymes to tunes I know?' She asked. 'They can be as bawdy as you like - no doubt that would please the company.'

'It would,' I said, as the notion struck home. 'Makan has no singing voice these days, little more than a croak, but he has skill with words – and he could dig out his old shawm to accompany me.' I gave her a smile, of mingled gratitude and relief. 'What a worthy friend you are, sweet Runa.'

'I'm not your sweet Runa,' she retorted, wiping the smile from my face. 'Nor am I pleased at the rumours that seem to abound from our meetings. I'm a chaste maid who's not about to spread her legs for a rake like you, Yorick. If I'm to teach you those tunes, I want something in return: that you quash the idle gossip concerning our relations. That shouldn't be difficult, since your usual habit is to boast shamelessly of your conquests. Are we in agreement?'

Well, I was subdued by that; gentle Runa, it transpired, had both pride and spirit. With a show of contrition, I made a bow and swore to meet her demand... and *confiteo*: to my consternation there came a warm stirring in my loins, that spoke of a desire I had never known regarding Runa. The notion of this well-shaped maid – I use her own words – spreading her legs for me was most delightful, and likely all the more tempting because it was a desire that could never be satisfied.

'In truth, I'm in your debt already,' I told her. 'And if you'll help me to three or four good tunes, I'll be indebted the more. Nor shall anyone be left thinking our meetings had any other purpose than to convey the Princess's wishes to Makan and me, regarding her father's needs.'

'That's well,' Runa said, though she looked less than satisfied. 'In any case, there's been little enough for you to tell. Dull tidings of soldiery and disbursements, and proclamations... I wonder whether Makan conceals real news for his master's sake – or more likely to safeguard his own neck, and yours.'

This was becoming difficult, and I rebuked myself for undervaluing Runa: she was the cleverest woman I knew, apart from Edela. I could not admit that her suspicions were correct: that Makan and I had kept to our plan of passing on only the most innocent fragments of the King's private talk, often making whole cloth out of scraps. The troubling thought arose that Princess Gurutha would start to suspect, and that Yorick would suffer for it.

'Then, I suppose there's little use in my telling of the Polack envoy coming to visit,' I said ruefully.

'No use whatsoever,' Runa answered. 'And now I'm going inside before I freeze to death. Meet me two days hence, and I'll teach you the tunes I know'.

We parted, and I went up to the chamber. There I set about making up a ballad about a stable boy and his mistress, with much wordplay on rutting and riding, before dismissing it: Makan would likely scorn my attempts as a rhymer. It was evening by then, and having seen nothing of him all day I ventured down to the kitchens in search of a supper. Makan, I learned, was still with the King, who was in sore need of comfort and diversion. For it seemed grave news had come from the west: Lord Gerwendil was dead.

I heard this from still-plump Ragnhild, who now ruled the kitchen maids. Taking a moment from her duties, she sat with me and told of the King's grief for his old friend, at whose side he had fought many a battle. Gerwendil left two grown sons, who would now govern Jutland together until Rorik decided otherwise.

'The brothers hate each other, it's said,' Ragnhild told me. 'They're as different as heron and hawk. Then, if they come to Kronborg in their father's stead you'll likely get to see them at close quarters, unlike the rest of us.'

My mind busy, I said nothing. This news, I realised, could shed a new light on the forthcoming banquet, hence I needed to speak with Makan. With a show of passing interest, I drew Ragnhild to speak of more trifling matters – until she stood up with a frown and placed her hands upon her hips.

'Stuffed with your own thoughts as always, master *hofnar*,' she sighed. 'You haven't even noticed my condition, though it's been plain enough for weeks - let alone congratulated Trostann on his coming fatherhood.'

I blinked, staring at her swollen belly, then put on my chastened look.

'Your pardon,' I said. 'I'm... I'm most happy for you both. When is, er...?'

'Three months or thereabouts, Hertha says. She has one of her own, you may recall, and is schooled in the matter of child-bearing.'

Confiteo: Yorick flinched at that. His memory of bedding the lusty Hertha, and her sister Hella too, was not so far back. For a moment he even harboured the thought that he might be the father of... no, that wouldn't do. I had much to concern myself with, and such speculation could lead to a kind of madness. Ragnhild was looking hard at me; our days of exchanging private smiles, following the unforgettable tryst in the brewing-house, were far behind.

'I wish you and your child good health,' I said. 'I'll try to drop a word in the King's ear, that he might send you something, and Trostann too-'

'Don't trouble yourself, Yorick,' Ragnhild said, cutting me short. 'We'll shift for ourselves. Doubtless you've grander things on your mind, mixing with the high-born folk as you do.'

She turned away from me and went off to her work. As my eyes followed her, I saw the other maids looking in my direction, sour-faced Thura among them. Perhaps only then did it strike me that with my new status at Makan's side, not to mention my huddled conferences with Runa, I had lost my place in the lowborn world from which I sprang. It seemed as though I dwelt in a kind of middle-land: a discomforting thought, that drove me to my feet and out of the room, leaving my supper unfinished.

But that night, after I helped Makan up the stairs to our chamber, I became engrossed in talk that drove the unsettling interlude in the kitchens from my thoughts. And I'm compelled to recall the other ones whose lives would be bound up with mine: those two brothers, one of whom would one day be my king.

The late Gerwendil's sons were named Horwendil and Feng or Fengr - *Fangen*, 'the fang' some called him, on account of a stray dog-tooth that showed at his upper lip. This was a clever and subtle lord, as Makan put it: sweet-voiced and sharp-witted, skilled in laws and counsel and in husbanding the wealth of his father's lands. But he was no great warrior, and there seemed little doubt in most minds which one our King would favour as the future ruler of Jutland: the sea rover Horwendil, slayer of the King of Norway and hero of many another exploit - a man after Rorik's heart.

'You know the story,' Makan said, sitting by our fire with a mug of warmed ale in his fist. 'How Old Norway considered himself rightful lord of the seaways and forced the young Horwendil to meet him in battle, over an island they disputed. How Horwendil went further and challenged the King to single combat, knowing full well that he was somewhat aged for such, but could not refuse for fear of being branded a coward. Hence, the outcome was never in much doubt.'

I nodded, remembering the tales of Horwendil's victory; how he had discarded his shield and gripped his adversary's sword in both hands, ignoring the blood that flowed. But after he had vanquished the Norwegian King, splitting his shield asunder and killing him with sword-thrusts, instead of scorning his enemy he had held him in respect, and ordered a proper burial. For this and other deeds he was admired throughout Denmark – not least by our King Rorik, when Horwendil sent gifts and spoils of war to his overlord. And now both brothers, the rival sons of old Gerwendil, would be honoured guests at the banquet, which was to be the most lavish occasion seen at Kronborg in a long while – and which brought Yorick and his almost-father to the nub of the matter: their own part in the entertainment.

'The King could command his players to return, from wherever they are,' Makan said. 'I advised him to do so, but he wouldn't agree. It seems that while one of the brothers – Feng, that is – would delight in seeing them perform, the other has no liking for such. He's a man among men, who'll have songs of battle and other heroic stuff – hence we must be ready.'

I had been impatient to tell him of my plan to learn Runa's tunes, to which he could put new words, but now I was disappointed. 'You mean Horwendil is one of austere tastes?' I asked. 'Are there to be no jests about fumbling and fucking?'

'Not so many as in the past,' Makan said, turning his rheumy eyes upon me. 'And it'd do you no harm to think less about those for once, and instead take the trouble to learn some of the ancient sagas... my memory's not what it was.'

'You can still fashion a rhyme,' I argued. 'Which is what I would talk of – Runa is to teach me some tunes to which new lines may be fitted, to suit the King's tastes. What do you say to that?'

A yawn welled up, which Makan didn't trouble to hide. He took a long pull from his mug, then: 'You mean I would fashion the songs, and you would sing them?'

I nodded eagerly. 'I can hit the notes, and you could play your shawm, to drown out any I miss.'

'I haven't played that in years,' Makan said. 'My fingers are too stiff... I couldn't even manage a pipe and tabor, as the English do.'

'Then don't,' I replied, in exasperation. 'Just be the balladeer you always were, and make me some verses to work with.'

He was silent, and seeing him falling into one of his morose humours, I sought to cheer him. 'The King will want us to look our best for the feast,' I said. 'Shall we ask for new livery – say a gaudy cap and bells, as the English jesters wear? We could raise a chuckle with those.'

Makan grimaced. 'I'll have none of that,' he muttered. 'But your notion of singing new songs to old tunes is fair. I'll apply myself to it, but now I'm for my bed.'

I was much reassured. 'We could make up a heroic song or two to please the Lord Horwendil,' I said eagerly, 'and bawdier stuff for the rest...' but seeing the look on his face, I trailed off.

'Do you still say the *mareridt* never visits you, Erik?' he asked, before turning away to stare into the fire. 'She comes to me, more and more.'

I shook my head; nightmares back then were all but unknown to Yorick, who slept like a corpse. Though I was sometimes aware that Makan tossed and mumbled in the night, so that when he rose he was sluggish from lack of sleep. Yet when I asked him if he would speak of the dreams the *mareridt* brought, he was unwilling.

'You knew hard toil, back when you were in the stables,' he murmured. 'But I tell you, there's no harder work than being a royal fool all day and most of the night too, with never an hour to yourself except for sleeping. Even the King, though he claims to love me, fails to notice my weariness. Remember that, when I'm gone and it falls to you to please him.'

'Sheep-shit, as our master would say,' I grinned, trying to shake him from this gloom. 'Despite what he ordered that time, you'll survive him, and I'll plead your case to the Princess for your retirement from the Court. Then you can sit before the fire and rest your old bones, for the remainder of your days.'

'I think not, Erik,' Makan said. 'And as for the Princess, if she marries the man I believe she will, you'll find her harder to please than ever.'

'What, has the King spoken of her betrothal already?' I asked.

'We'll talk of it later...' He yawned again. 'Will you let me to my bed?'

Well now: in a state of some excitement, Yorick soon forgot Makan's words and set himself to learn the tunes Runa taught him, standing in the cold behind the brewing-house wall, the place being locked up at that time. To her satisfaction I was a quick learner, and was soon able to hum and *tra-la* the fair melodies that came from far-off France and Italy, brought by wandering balladeers to the cold shores of Denmark. After our second lesson she pronounced me fluent enough and returned indoors, wrapped in her winter gown with her hands tucked into the sleeves. In good spirits I followed her into the castle, walking at what I believed was a safe distance behind, until she turned into the broad passageway that led to the presence chamber. Going that way, I see now, was one of the biggest mistakes of Yorick's life; but he was careless that day, humming a tune and daring to admire Runa's firm rump as she drew further ahead – until he was brought to an abrupt halt. Without warning, out of a doorway stepped the Princess

Gurutha with two young serving-maids at her heels. There was a moment of recognition, the Princess' gaze flying from Runa to myself and back, before a familiar shriek froze me to the bone.

Runa was the first to feel Gurutha's wrath: hurrying to her mistress she curtsied, murmuring words I couldn't hear but assumed to be of apology. The response was a blow cracked across Runa's face, delivered with such force that she was knocked sideways. There followed a shouted instruction to depart, which she obeyed with alacrity. Then, while I stood wishing the floor would split asunder and deliver me into some deep pit, the Princess advanced upon me at such a pace that her servants were hard pressed to keep up.

'You vile lump of shit!' Gurutha screamed into my face. 'Do you think me such a dimwit that I don't know what goes on under my own roof? When you flirt with my maid like a rutting boar? You think you can scorn me, sniggering with the King like the hop-toad you are, quaffing his wine like a favourite? More, you dare flout my orders and fail to do what I-'

Just in time she stopped herself: in her rage she had almost spoken of our secret before the two maids, who were trembling in fear. Mastering herself, which took some effort, Gurutha turned swiftly and dismissed them. Then, her chest rising and falling under its weight of brocade and jewels, she waited until they were out of earshot.

'Come with me,' she ordered.

I followed her along the passage, past a stone-faced sentry who bowed and gave such a show of ignorance of what he'd just witnessed, I had to admire his skill. Through a doorway we went and along another passage, until we arrived at a small windowed chamber which was seldom used and empty of furnishings. Telling me to close the door, the Princess allowed me to approach her and make my bow, my face a mask of servility. I rose quickly, whereupon her ringed hand shot out to grasp me about the throat.

'You've been lying to me, Yorick,' she said in a voice of ice.

'By the gods I swear I have not, Highness,' I gulped.

'Liar! I know that you and Runa have met without my leave – do you deny it?'

'I do… no, that is, we met today so that she could teach me some tunes,' I stammered. 'So that I may sing at the banquet-'

'You've been seen lusting after her – in brazen disobedience to my orders,' Gurutha broke in. 'Do you think you're the only one who spies for me?'

The kitchen maids; most likely Thura, I thought, cursing her silently. Pummelling my mind for something to say, I drew a breath but was forestalled.

'I warned you, if you ever touched Runa I would make you suffer! You forget your sworn service to me – and you've even failed in that! Do you know what it is I speak of?'

'Highness, I swear I've reported all that I've heard, faithfully and without embellishment,' I answered, as earnestly as I dared. 'My only desire has been to inform you of anything that touches on your…'

I stopped, swallowing my words as the truth dawned: now I recalled Makan's tired speech of two days before: *if the Princess marries the man I believe she will…* and my asking him if the King had spoken of her betrothal. In my eagerness to meet with Runa, the matter had slipped from my thoughts. Feeling somewhat sick, I met Gurutha's eye and saw her look of mingled anger and triumph as, at last, she withdrew her hand from my throat.

'Well?' She demanded. 'Do you deny that you failed to tell me of my father's intentions toward me, regarding the Lords of Jutland?'

'I cannot, Highness,' I replied, my mouth dry as sand. 'In truth Makan began to tell me something a while ago, yet he was weary, and I didn't know he-'

'Stop!' Gurutha shouted, almost spitting in my face. 'Do you think I give a fart for your excuses? The most important tidings ever, that could shape my whole future as Queen - and you fail to deliver them! What other matters have you neglected to report? You wretch - I've a mind to have you whipped, and banished from the kingdom!'

I was silent, berating myself for a clod who could win tournaments over every clod in Denmark. Now the import of

Makan's words was clear: Rorik had talked to him in private, of offering Gurutha's hand in marriage to either Horwendil or Feng in tribute to their father, his old and much-lamented friend. Had Makan truly forgotten to tell me of it the next morning – was his mind so fuddled? Then, I too was to blame... like a careless potboy destined for a flogging, I hung my head.

'Look at me!' Gurutha cried. 'I demand your answer – what else have you failed to tell me?'

'Nothing, I swear,' I said, though no longer certain of it. 'I've heard naught about the Lords of Jutland except what everyone knows, of their coming to the feast. If you'll give me leave, I'll go at once to Makan and – no, I'll beg an audience with the King and-'

'Stop, again!' To my consternation, Gurutha raised her hand and clapped it over my mouth. 'Enough of your babbling. They say you could charm a starving wolf from eating you – somewhat like your friend Sveinn, that man-maid of a player. I've even heard you let him fondle you, or worse – is that true?'

'Highness, upon my life I swear it's not,' I exclaimed, my thoughts whirling – was that Thura again, spreading more lies? 'I would never do such...'

I stopped: Gurutha was looking intently at me now. Her anger seemed to have subsided, to be replaced with... what? No - it was madness to think such. At once I recalled that spring morning in the King's garden, when I'd been so dull-witted as to think she was being coquettish towards me. I stifled a cough, pleading silently to whatever gods there were that she would send me away, to a flogging or worse. I cared not – until:

'Then, what do you do?' The Princess enquired. 'And with whom? Not Runa,' she added, before I could answer. 'I know her better than you do, whatever lustful thoughts you harbour. Who, pray, is your latest conquest, Master Yorick?'

'Highness... I beg you not to sully yourself with such talk,' I gulped; *confiteo*, at her words my cock had shrunk to the size of a bean. 'Servants' ways are not those of princes...'

'Yet you know that's not always so,' Gurutha said, with a look that struck fear into my heart. 'My own father's behaviour has in the past given rise to much lewd talk – or do you pretend not to have heard?'

'I... I cannot say,' I said, sinking into misery. 'Please let me know your will, and I'll obey at once – even to quitting the kingdom as you said.' Whereupon, drained of responses, I shut my mouth and awaited my fate. But when it came, I almost sagged at the knees.

'My will?' the Princess Gurutha said. 'Well, in view of how desperate you are to serve me, will this do for an answer?'

Upon which – and I swear it is the unvarnished truth – she took my face in both hands, pulled it down to hers and kissed me hard upon the mouth, lingering there until I gasped for breath.

'There now,' she sighed, drawing away. 'Will you show me your skill, so that I may see for myself how you've earned your reputation? I demand that you serve me, here and now. So - which of us should go first? Do I lift my gown, or will you?'

NINE

Of course I did not! Damnation and derision upon anyone who thinks otherwise. The future Queen, who could have had me hung by the wrists until my arms were stretched to rags, or hanged, or boiled alive in a cauldron, as I heard an English king did to the cook who tried to poison him? This is Gurutha I speak of: the harpy in broidered silk who would henceforth be my bane – who is so still, as I lie here. And I've sworn to tell all, have I not? Then, hear the truth of what transpired in that dusty room on a winter's day when the hapless, cock-shrivelled Yorick stood before the Princess and heard the invitation which, coming from any other mouth than hers, would have been a cause for delight, but instead filled him with dread.

'Highness, you know I must not,' I whispered. 'I dare not.'

'You forget your place,' Gurutha countered, with a smile that bordered on a sneer. 'Your duty is to serve me - and I wish to learn carnality, so that I might please my future husband. I'm tired of dwelling in ignorance – I order you to do my bidding.'

'But I cannot. It... it would be wrong,' I stammered, shaking my head. 'A princess should go to her bridal bed chaste and unsullied - and besides, her husband would know if she'd-'

'What, do you think I don't know that?'

Gurutha cut me short, her smile gone and her chest heaving with anger. 'After all this time you still think me a child,' she snapped, 'and I'll have none of it. I've ordered you to pleasure your future Queen – do you dare disobey me?'

'I must, Highness,' I whined. 'It would be utterly remiss of me – even treasonous, and in time you'll be glad I refused. Give me another order, I pray – whatever it be, I'll carry it out to the letter.'

Silence fell, and for a moment I believed she would strike me as she had poor Runa: she lifted her hand and I braced myself for the blow, but none came. Instead she put her palm to my cheek, and pressed it there. I was abashed – and in sudden doubt: had this been some kind of a trial? Of loyalty, or affection, or…

'Am I to take it you don't find me alluring?' she enquired.

'By the gods no, it's not… I swear, any man would,' I blustered. 'But please understand, I'm unworthy of you…'

'You can't do it, can you,' Gurutha said, her voice flat. 'Despite your famed prowess, when faced with one of my station you're limp as a melted candle.'

I swallowed, drowning the protest that threatened to spring to my lips. In truth she was correct, but it chafed me to hear my manhood impugned so. I managed a nod.

'Well then…' She withdrew her hand and took a step backwards, wearing a sly look. 'What if you had done what I asked?' she enquired. 'Or I might say, what if I let it be known that you had tried?'

Confiteo: at that, real fear gripped Yorick - a bowel-loosening fear that spread from his gut to his extremities. Surely, she wouldn't do that? I reasoned. Would it not bring more shame upon her than on me – unless she accused me of…

'You understand me, I think,' Gurutha said, in that steely tone she liked to use. 'We're alone here, yet we were seen together. What did or did not take place is known only to the two of us – and who would take the word of the rogue Yorick over mine? Not my father - you may wager a king's ransom on that.'

My body had turned to ice; I waited, in full knowledge of the sway she held over me; this time, my life really did hang in the balance.

'And yet…' one of those half-smiles appeared, and a faint hope sparked within me. That demon Gurutha - upon my life, how she relished it: power, bright and untarnished. 'And yet,' she repeated, 'I'm loth to make such an accusation. Did you truly think me so cruel?'

'No, I… of course not, Highness,' I breathed, judging this a moment for flattery of the most brazen kind. 'And I swear, my love and devotion to you are undimmed - I ask your pardon, if I've ever given you reason to think I could-'

'Enough,' Gurutha broke in – and for a brief moment I could almost hear her father; she was Rorik's daughter, when all was said and sifted. 'Save your sugared words, and spin them for your next conquest. Listen to me now, and listen well.'

At once I was most attentive, as she laid forth her instructions.

'You'll continue to be my ears at the Court, whenever I'm absent,' the Princess announced, in measured fashion. 'Especially with regard to talk of the sons of Gerwendil. I want every scrap of knowledge about the brothers relayed to me...' she sighed with impatience. 'I suppose it must always come by tongue, through Runa. A plague on you and your ignorance – can't you even write your name?'

With a show of shame, I replied that I could not.

'Very well...' she took a breath, straightened herself and held out her hand for me to kiss. And when that was done, and I had hurried to open the door for her, she swept out into the passage without a backward glance. Whereupon her limp rag of a servant, her excuse for an intelligencer, her impotent clown Yorick backed into the room until he fetched up by a wall, where he sat down in the dust to recover his wits.

Henceforth, I knew, I must not be remiss while the Princess Gurutha lived, but be alert at every moment. You stop moving, you die... and I had no wish to die just yet.

The day of the banquet was fast approaching, and Makan and I were ready. But first let me speak of the songs, for I was proud of those, and am still.

There were four of them: one an old drinking song which Makan could manage, drawing the company into a rousing chorus, and which owed nothing to the fair tunes Runa had taught me. We would save it for the latter part of the feast, he said, when the wine had flowed enough to loosen both tongues and purse-strings. The other songs, however, would give me my chance to shine, not only before the King but before his guests. For there was no doubting now, at

Kronborg and beyond, that Rorik intended to make proclamation before the assembled company, the lords and landsmen of all Denmark: not only concerning his choice as ruler of Jutland, but also with regard to the betrothal of his daughter. Among gamesters, Horwendil was the clear favourite for her hand, but others spoke of Rorik's habit of confounding everyone by making unlikely decisions: in short, of doing the unexpected.

'Anyone who thinks the King a fool is a double fool himself,' Makan said to me. 'He will choose Feng, for he values other qualities besides fighting skills: a mind filled with knowledge for one, along with a sharp wit and a worldly manner.'

'Well, you're living proof,' I said. 'A baseborn serf who by Rorik's will has become a favoured companion, closer to the throne than most.'

'And is hated for it by some,' Makan observed with a dour look. 'I've warned you to be vigilant – the higher you rise, the more enemies you will make.'

'You have,' I agreed, eager to move away from this tiresome talk. 'Now, can I sing for you again?'

He nodded, and I launched into a melancholy song set to one of Runa's tunes, about a youth who goes to war and leaves his lover distraught, waiting for his return. After he's been away a long time, she receives the news that he's fallen in battle and drowns herself. Then her lover returns wounded, and is grief-stricken. But he's a fierce warrior now, and henceforth he vows never to marry but to make his enemies pay with their lives, for the rest of his days. I ended the song with a kind of battle-cry, my fist raised in defiance, and looked to Makan for approval – only to see him frowning.

'Did I fashion all of that? I don't recall it.'

'The rhyme isn't exactly as you gave it to me,' I admitted. 'I altered it somewhat, thinking it would please the Lord Horwendil.'

'I suppose it might. But I'd lose the end – that shouting and flailing about. Any soldier would laugh at it, which isn't the intent.'

'Very well,' I said, somewhat peeved. 'Shall I sing the others? They're unchanged - or one of them is, the one about the King's father, the mighty Hother. The other, the song about the *huldra*... I've altered that a little, too.'

'Have you now?' My almost-father gave me one of his looks. 'Why would you want to do that?'

Seeing his displeasure, I hesitated. In truth there was nothing wrong with the rhyme he'd fashioned, about a young man who meets the legendary *huldra*: the wild but beautiful half-maiden, half-beast, with a tail which she hides when she encounters mortals. In an attempt to please Gurutha, however, knowing she would sit beside her father at the feast, I'd made it into a more daring tale of seduction, in which the youth tries to woo the creature but comes to a terrible end for his boldness - strangled by the very appendage she hid from him. But when I explained this to Makan he scoffed.

'Do you truly think the Princess would enjoy such fare?' He demanded. 'It sounds like a warning to her suitors, to be wary of what they pursue.'

'Does it?' I wondered; my encounter with Gurutha was still raw, and I was too ashamed to tell Makan of it. 'That wasn't my purpose. You know how she likes a surprise – a twist in the tale. Here it's a twist in the *tail* too... you follow?'

'By the gods, Erik,' he sniffed. 'Sing the ballad about the maid who drowns herself, if you will, and the one about old King Hother - but leave the last song as winsome as I made it. The *huldra* isn't known for strangling folk. Nor do we want to send the entire company into a gloom – this is to be a night of joy and celebration, have you forgotten?'

Somewhat deflated, I submitted to his will. But when I pondered the matter later I saw that, as always, Makan was right. So: in the time left to us we practised our jests and clowning more than I did my singing, and the song of the *huldra* remained as he had penned it.

And then, quite suddenly the great day was upon us.

Kronborg was transformed: from the sleepy castle it was in winter, apart from at Yuletide, to a place of bustle and excitement decked with hangings and banners. Lords came from all over the realm, along with their ladies and their trains, so that the stables were soon filled and horses had to be placed in outbuildings, even in Helsingor where the inns too were full. Laughter and conversation filled the place, old friends were reunited, young blades found maidens to charm. And in the afternoon before the banquet, with a dusting of snow on the hard ground, the Lord Horwendil arrived attended by a small guard of armed men and servants laden with gifts. And, *confiteo*: Yorick took one look at him, and felt his spirits drop. Here, he judged, was a man without humour: a proud, unsmiling commander who, if he indeed became ruler of Jutland and – more importantly in my eyes – was given Gurutha's hand in marriage, would bring her to a life of duty, and likely of joyless and constant motherhood. But the notion that troubled me most was that if she went to live in her husband's castle in the west, she might want to take me along as her fool. It seems plain conceit now that I should think so - and besides, I was mistaken; but I leap ahead again.

We were in the presence chamber, Makan and myself, mingling with the assembled counsellors and attendants when Horwendil made his entrance, striding in dignified manner to the throne and making a stiff bow to the King. The Princess, splendidly attired, was at his side upon her own chair. Rorik spoke words of welcome which I was too far away to hear, but which Horwendil accepted gravely. He was a tall man, full-bearded and half-armoured as if for battle – which, it struck me afterwards, was indeed the case in that he and his brother, who was yet unseen by anyone at Kronborg, were bitter rivals: both for high office and for the hand of Gurutha. Musing on this, I saw Makan making his way towards me, and understood that we should get closer to the throne. This we did, threading our way through the silent watchers until we were in earshot.

'You are the first to arrive, my good friend,' Rorik was saying. 'What of the Lord Feng? Is he delayed?'

'I regret, I cannot answer for my brother, Highness,' Horwendil said, his mouth somewhat taut. 'He swore he would be here, but nowadays his actions seem subject to every passing whim.' Whereupon, with deliberate slowness, he turned towards the Princess and bowed again. 'Lady Gurutha... what a glad day is this, one that I feared would never arrive. Please accept this token of my devotion, which I have kept close to my heart. I hope you will always wear it, whatever comes to us.'

There was a murmur from the assembled company as Horwendil bent his knee, drew an object from his tunic and held it out across both hands: a fine chain of gold with jewelled roundels, which Gurutha cordially accepted. Approval showed on Rorik's face, and remained while his guest spoke of other gifts he had brought, which he would show later. For the present, he announced, he wished to thank the King for his messages of condolence on the death of his lamented father Gerwendil, staunch friend of Rorik. The loss was keenly felt by all, he reported - even though, Horwendil confessed, he'd had little time to mourn since the business of government pressed so hard upon him. To which Makan and I exchanged smirks: for all his loftiness, it appeared, the lord had lost no time in jousting for supremacy, letting it be known that he was hard-working and diligent, while his brother...

'We'll speak of that,' Rorik said, cheerfully enough. 'But cast aside your cares - today's a holiday, a time for feasting... and song.' This with a glance at his fools, who had shuffled to the front of the crowd wearing wide grins. 'We've taken pains to make this our grandest occasion, at which our daughter too shall preside... will you walk with us now, while we show you the splendours of Kronborg?' To which invitation Horwendil readily assented, the King and Gurutha rose and the watchers made way, bowing as the royal party passed. As he walked by Makan and me, Rorik turned aside and spoke low.

'I count on you tonight,' he muttered. 'Disappoint me, and I'll have you both gelded.'

A short time later the two of us went outdoors to gather our thoughts, clutching mugs of ale we'd begged from the kitchen – now a madhouse of frenzied activity, filled with steam and shouting and the odour of roasting meat. In the main courtyard, where others had gathered to take the cool air, there was gossip and speculation - the chief topic being, when would Lord Feng come? His tardiness was seen by some as an affront to the King, by others as mere carelessness, but wiser heads – Makan among them - held a different view: that Horwendil's brother was too clever to make a mistake of such magnitude. His entrance was planned, Makan maintained, to raise curiosity and hence to gain attention.

'Observe him at close hand when he comes,' he advised me. 'For this could be the one you will serve after I'm gone, if he wins the Princess's hand.'

'I doubt that,' I answered. 'Did you see the way the King looked on Lord Horwendil? There's his future son-in-law – I'd wager on it.'

'Then you're fortunate I never gamble,' Makan grunted. ''Else your purse would soon be empty.'

We walked the courtyard, our heads filled with thoughts of the banquet, and in Yorick's case with apprehension for what would be his most important performance yet in the High Hall; few remembered his role as a maid-servant in *The Jealous Husband*. I had the songs by heart, but it was the banter and invention which troubled me, such as how to field the jeers and abuse I might attract from drunken revellers - something Makan excelled at. I might be pelted, I knew, with crusts of bread or worse: someone had once poured a flagon of Rhenish over Makan, at which he'd licked his lips and pronounced it too stale, winning delighted applause. But uppermost in my thoughts was the business of pleasing Gurutha and her suitors, who would take the places of honour on either side of the King. Whichever of the two brothers found himself next to the Princess was likely to be the favoured one - and hence, this was the man we should seek to please, Makan said. Should it be Horwendil, too many bawdy jests might go amiss; should it be the Lord Feng, he guessed, songs of war and heroism might fall equally flat.

'Read both brothers,' Makan instructed me, 'as you might read a book if you could, and strive to suit your performance to their humours. It's not the common company we must satisfy – a pox on them if they grow restive – but the High Table. Remember to pitch your voice towards them, so as-'

'I know it,' I muttered. 'I think of little else. Mayhap you should raise your own voice a pitch – it's not so strong as it was.'

The light was fading now, as we drained our mugs and made ready to go indoors, whereupon there was a stir from across the courtyard. A sentry called down from the wall, and men hurried towards the gatehouse; there was a buzz of voices, the cause of which soon became clear: Lord Feng had arrived at last.

And so, Yorick had sight of another one whose affairs would in time be enmeshed with his own; if only he had been ready.

The Fang, as in private I would call him, rode easily through the gates of Kronborg on a splendid chestnut horse, itself arrayed with the finest of trappings, his fur cloak spread behind him as if he had stopped outside to arrange it. A company of liveried servants followed, brightly dressed as if for a summer fair rather than for winter. And though it may have been the gathering dusk that hampered my view of Feng, I swear the man wore the broadest smile I've ever seen. This was not the face of an earnest suitor, I thought, nor that of a supplicant lord come to plead for office: it was the look of a man who believed he had already gained both, and was here to collect his due reward.

Standing in the cold, I watched courtiers jostle to be first to welcome the newcomer - including many who had hitherto sworn Horwendil was the favoured one. Such is the nature of fealty: people will flock towards the fire, eager to share in its warmth. And to the eyes of Kronborg's jesters Feng, sitting on his fine horse and smiling down upon those who gathered about him, was most practised in the art of radiating warmth when it suited him. Not only that: having picked his moment, the great lord produced a purse, opened it and drew out a handful of coins which he proceeded to scatter among the crowd. And I swear I saw him smirk, at the alacrity with which men stooped to gather them up.

I looked at Makan, who was gazing at the new arrival without expression, until he bent his head close to my ear.

'As I said, you're fortunate I don't gamble,' he murmured. Upon which, instead of joining the welcoming party, he turned about and went indoors.

But Yorick stayed, and wondered.

TEN

Well now, what a momentous night that was: one which was talked of forever after, throughout all Denmark. The one on which several men's futures were decided; the one on which the Princess Gurutha left her girlhood behind and took her place in the affairs of the realm; and the one on which Yorick stepped out of Makan's shadow to become the Favoured Fool at Rorik's court. But first let me speak further of the sons of Gerwendil, rivals for the Princess's hand and honoured guests at the feast, who were also the bitterest of enemies.

That evening, in the short hours before the banquet, rumours flew about Kronborg. The Lord Feng had at last presented himself to the King, it was told, and enjoyed an audience with him and with Gurutha, leading to much speculation. The King had been somewhat cool towards him, some said, while others insisted their meeting was warm, with Feng offering fine gifts to the Princess. More, he had brought with him a great sheaf of charts and documents showing the wealth and condition of Jutland, with suggestions for improvements he wished to make – improvements, Feng reported sadly, which his brother had declined to consider, being so set in his ways. Horwendil, during this time, was still being shown the sights of Kronborg by the King's chamberlain, and was observed to be ill-at-ease on being told of his brother's arrival.

All of this and more was heard by Makan and I as we braced ourselves with mugs of ale in a corner of the kitchen, waiting to be called to entertain. The banquet had begun, with a procession of servants carrying platters of food and stoups of wine into the High Hall. The noise of the company, being close by, filled our ears, and to my surprise Makan was taut. That my almost-father, veteran of countless such feasts, should be fretting was the last thing I wished to see. Hence, knowing that it was my place to cheer him now, I ran through a few rhymes to distract him. The one about the cow that farted perfume had always been a favourite, but even that fell flat.

'I've heard it too often,' he growled, 'but then, it's not me you have to amuse. You tell it well enough – work your way towards the High Table, and leave me to the lesser folk.'

I nodded and lifted my mug – and on a sudden, our waiting was over. A servant appeared with the order: The King would have his fools attend him. So we rose, Makan downing his ale at a gulp, and hurried to the High Hall, capering into its blaze of candlelight; or rather, I capered while Makan stumbled after me as best he could. And from that moment Yorick had no time for nervousness but fell eagerly into his part: it was that, or the devil would take him.

At first we clowned and bantered at will, swiping courtiers' hats and changing them for our own, with antic jests about swollen heads and baldness. Makan worked one long table, I another, throwing in rhymes where it suited. There was some laughter, and many an insult thrown our way, though some of the guests ignored us or were even annoyed by our presence, their eyes ever fixed on the High Table. As I moved among them, stealing a sip of wine here or a morsel of food there, my eyes strayed towards the King's party - and on observing the seating placements, I soon veered towards Makan's view as to who was most favoured by Rorik. As expected, the brothers were on either side of him – but it was Feng who sat beside Gurutha, and was most attentive towards her. Indeed, the more glances I stole, the stronger grew my belief that there was an attraction between the Princess and the smiling latecomer. Despite the dog-tooth that protruded he was a handsome man, richly dressed, neatly coiffed and shaven, with delicate hands that seemed forever busy, refilling the Princess's cup or offering her some choice dish. Moreover, one look at the face of the great sea rover Horwendil showed that he was only too aware of the business. While he conversed with Rorik, his eyes moved often towards Gurutha and to his brother, who was exerting the full weight of his charms upon her - and cared not a whit who saw it.

The Princess, of course, revelled in the attention. She glowed: never had I seen her look so fine or indeed so womanly, in a new gown and many jewels – though not the gold chain Horwendil had gifted her. Her hair was carefully dressed, bound with a circlet of silver. And though from time to time she spoke with her father, she rarely looked beyond him to her other suitor, and such glances grew fewer as time passed.

By now, Makan was entertaining favoured guests at the top end of the long table that lay square to the King's: knights and courtiers who were already loud with drink. The noise in the hall swelled as servants moved about with flagons and more platters of food. And soon, to my alarm I realised that Makan was somewhat drunk. The renowned jester, it seemed, who'd told me how he always resisted the King's encouragement to get soused, had thrown aside his own advice and succumbed to a surfeit of wine. I would have gone to draw him into some clowning, whereupon I saw him pull a joined-stool away from the table. Heads turned as Makan clambered unsteadily atop it, and began to declaim to the company at large.

'Pray listen, gentles all!' He shouted. 'Will you hear our tribute, to the late father of our beloved monarch? Bend your ears to the sweet voice of Yorick, who will sing of the mighty Hother.' He turned towards the King. 'Is it your will, sire? Has Yorick leave to sing the ballad he's studied so hard - for if not, I fear his head will burst with the import of it!'

There was a murmur of laughter, which died away as all eyes went to the King. Some also looked in my direction, as I faced the High Table in anticipation. There was a moment, before Rorik raised a hand for silence.

'He shall sing for us, Master Makan,' the King said graciously. 'But first I suggest you climb down from your perch, before you fall off it.'

'As you please, Highness,' Makan called back. 'Though were I to fall upon my arse, I'll not be the only one to do so this night – no names,' he added quickly, with a grin at the honoured guests. The jest, of course, was understood, and there was a ripple of surprise at his effrontery, along with a few suppressed laughs.

But the King remained impassive, extending a hand in my direction. A hush fell as Yorick came forward, took a space near to the High Table and sang his ballad of Hother. It was a stirring tale of past glories, but set to one of Runa's tunes it had a sweetness that could have made it a lament, save that it ended on a note of triumph and of praise for Rorik, the son of whom Hother would be proud. I finished, drawing out my last note until it died away, lowered my head in due reverence – and drew breath as, mercifully, applause rang out. To my relief, it was heartening: there were cries, there was banging on tables - even Gurutha looked impressed. The King was smiling, while on either side of him his guests showed their approval in different ways. Horwendil the warrior nodded gravely... and Feng?

Feng was looking hard at me, with a smile that appeared forced. At first I feared the song was not to his taste, or had gone on too long... or was he still surprised by Makan's insolence? I saw him lean towards Gurutha and whisper – at which she too smiled, quite demurely. But they both looked in my direction, and to my embarrassment Gurutha put a hand to her lips and blew me a kiss, sending it on its way with a wave. I smiled and bowed - but once again, the Princess had struck fear into my heart.

I own you, she was saying, *and I always will.*

Thereafter, the evening rolled on until it roared.

Makan struggled to keep his wits, while continuing to steal a drink now and again until I feared he would fall, as he'd said himself, on his rump. Meanwhile the King grew somewhat fuddled too, which was rare for a man of his capacity, laughing loudly at the rhymes his jesters declaimed – even the one about the cow that farted perfume, old and hoary as it was. So that when it came to my song of the maiden and her lover who went off to war, I feared it was too maudlin for the prevailing humour, but I was wrong: the King applauded with vigour, to which everyone else followed suit... and all the while, the Lord Horwendil's countenance darkened as he watched his brother's shameless wooing of the Princess Gurutha.

And quite suddenly it seemed as though the night had flown, and King Rorik had as yet made no proclamation.

It was late, so late that candles were being replaced, stomachs were stuffed and many a man had drunk to excess. In truth it was like old times, when Yorick was a boy and the noise of Rorik's carousing would wake him in the night, the Queen having retired in disgust; and Makan would be up until dawn, clowning until he was fit to drop. This night he had sung his drinking song, with no need to encourage the chorus: the High Hall shook to its roof as the entire company bellowed in unison; the fact that Makan himself was gloriously drunk seemed only to add to the pleasure.

We had both run out of rhymes, our voices were hoarse, and Yorick's only fear was that he would be called on to sing again. But by then such matters were all but forgotten, since there was barely a sober soul left apart from myself – and the favoured guests, those rival sons of Gerwendil. All show of cordiality was gone from Horwendil, who now sat with a face of thunder. He no longer looked at his brother or even at the Princess, and some who were nearby - those whose senses were not too dulled - began to grow wary of what might happen. And all the while Feng seemed not to notice, but continued his charming of Gurutha, who seemed more taken than ever by his attentions. Whereupon, when the banquet was threatening to sink into an occasion of either sullenness or debauchery, King Rorik chose the moment to get to his feet, startling everybody by calling loudly for silence. As the hall gradually stilled, somewhat tardily in places, he raised his hands and called again, until every face was turned in his direction, every bleary eye opened. He waited longer, until the silence was complete, and then spoke up.

'You know why you are present,' Rorik boomed - and I saw that he wasn't drunk at all, but had seemingly feigned it. 'We are moved to make known our choice as ruler of Jutland - and moreover, to give our daughter's hand in marriage to the noble lord in question. Much thought have we given to this above all other matters, for the good of our realm, that being of greater import than mere contentment of certain minds – like my fool, I name no names.'

He paused, his eyes scanning the hall, finally settling on Makan slumped at the end of a table, empty mug in hand. And in dismay, I knew what would happen: Makan tried to stand, only to collapse in a sodden heap.

And - I saw then that it was his last night of foolery; that the King was displeased and might even dismiss him – and the truth came blazing at me: Makan had willed it. He had shamed himself before all of Denmark, while at the same time presenting his almost-son: the young fool Yorick, who would take his place. But there was no time to think: heads were turning from Makan back to Rorik, as he spoke again.

'We have weighed the matter,' he declaimed, 'and have made our decision.' He paused again as if enjoying the hush, the way men strove to sober themselves in anticipation. The heirs of Gerwendil sat taut, eyes averted - and yet, beneath the solemn expression on Feng's face I believed I glimpsed a smile, one that he struggled to contain. Given all that I'd seen and heard since his arrival, not to say his being placed beside the Princess, the outcome now seemed obvious; looking about, I saw most people were of the same mind - hence, when the announcement came it was a thunderbolt.

'I name Horwendil, son of Gerwendil, ruler of Jutland,' Rorik proclaimed, his voice filling the hall. 'And he shall have the hand of my daughter, the Princess Gurutha. This is my word, and is not to be gainsaid.'

There was a collective gasp followed by a hush - but the King was not finished. Raising a hand again, he turned to Horwendil and placed the other hand upon his shoulder. 'And this too is my wish,' he continued, facing the company again. 'That when I'm gone to join my father in the after-world, Horwendil shall succeed me as King of all Denmark, and Gurutha shall be his Queen. I put it now to you, the elective nobles gathered here. So, my lords, will you stand and confirm it?'

His words came like the crack of doom. Many appeared shocked by the pronouncement: that the wilful Gurutha was not to depart with her future husband, but would in time rule here at Kronborg when the dour-faced Horwendil became King. Consternation rose, as minds befuddled with drink struggled to grasp the import of it. Some men looked resigned, others frowned or stared at their neighbours in disbelief. A muttering arose, which threatened to grow louder until one lord, more alert than most, had the presence of mind to voice his pleasure. This worthy stood up, lifting his cup in salute to the chosen successor: Horwendil, who himself looked chastened by the announcement. But as others began to get to their feet, raising their cups and calling out his name, the new ruler of Jutland stood to acknowledge the approval. He turned briefly to Rorik, who nodded and sat down. And soon, the whole company were offering toasts and applauding - notably those who had flocked to Feng's side but a few hours ago. All of this I saw, my gaze shifting from Horwendil to the King to the slighted one: Feng, who sat staring ahead, his face devoid of expression. Then at last my eyes settled on Gurutha, as did those of others, most curious to see her reaction.

My first thought was that she would fall into a swoon. Like Feng at her side, she too was very still, hands clasped tight as if to steady them. Then her eyes closed, and a shadow seemed to pass over her features. When she opened them again they were downcast, as if drawn to something on the table before her. She appeared to shrink within herself, and a weariness came upon her. At last she rose to her feet, murmured something inaudible and eyed a nearby attendant, who hurried to pull her chair back.

Without looking either to left or right, Gurutha left the High Table and walked to the doorway where, as if by design, two maids appeared to accompany her. She went out without a backward glance, leaving a silence in the hall. For a moment no-one seemed sure what to do – not even the King – until the spell was broken by Makan who, unnoticed by all, had recovered enough to get to his feet.

'All hail Queen Gurutha!' he yelled. 'Youth will have its day, and the old must withdraw to their firesides to prattle of what's past. A pox on all of you; go to your beds and sleep till doomsday for all I care - the King's will is done!' Whereupon he made a mocking bow and staggered towards the main doors, snatching a jug from the end of a table before disappearing from sight.

And there stood Yorick in turmoil, not knowing whether to make a discreet exit, or go to the King and ask to be dismissed, or pledge allegiance to the monarch-in-waiting. Yet when I looked about, I saw that the night was indeed over: folk were getting up, helping others to their feet, some making their way to the High Table to pay homage. To my relief Rorik himself rose, signalling that the feast was ended. Horwendil rose too and made to follow his future father-in-law, as servants ran to attend them both. Last to leave was Feng, who waited until the throng had thinned before making his own departure; no-one accosted him. When servants began clearing the bestrewn tables I left the Hall, but went not to the jesters' chamber, weary as I was. Instead I walked through departing revellers and their drink-slurred talk, and got myself outside into the freezing night.

For a while I stood, drinking in the sharp air, my thoughts whirling. Owls called, distant waves lashed the Sund far below, and from the stables came the snickering of restless horses. Lights still showed from the kitchen: few of those who toiled there would get to their beds before dawn. And on a sudden I pictured Gitte in her workaday frock, wiping sweat from her forehead with her good hand. Surely she would be content, I thought, to see me entertain the highborn, drawing their laughter with my foolery and charming them with my singing... wasn't it all she'd ever wanted for me?

I turned about and went indoors, making my way through the corridors and arches of Kronborg and thence to the stair that led to our chamber, only now remembering that I should have helped Makan up; someone else must have done so, since there was no sign of him. Hence it was with relief that, when I entered the room, I found him lying fully-clothed across his pallet, snoring and snorting like a dray-horse.

The chamber stank with his wine-breath, as I stumbled about in the faint glow of a rush-light. Tired to exhaustion I dragged a coverlet over Makan, then shrugged off my fool's clothing, shivering in the cold, and at last got myself into bed. I was determined not to think: thinking was for the morning, when both my almost-father and myself must face the future.

Whatever its shape, it would be different to what had gone before.

For a while I couldn't still my mind, busy as it was with the events of the night, but at last I drifted into a troubled sleep. Thereafter, like many of those at Kronborg, I slept long after sunrise, waking with a start to find the chamber filled with light. I sat up and looked across to Makan's pallet, to see him lying as I had left him, fully-dressed beneath the coverlet.

But he was no longer snoring; he was dead.

ELEVEN

Turn it about as you will, it was always thus: as one man falls another rises. Yet in those weeks that followed the death of one Yorick had truly loved, he was a boat adrift without steering-board or sight of land. He had lost not only his tutor and counsellor; he had lost his protector, the only man who could speak for him at the Court of Rorik Slyngebond: the King who had already named his successor, and was seemingly content to let majesty shift from him towards his daughter and her betrothed. And quite amazed was Yorick, to see how quickly it happened.

One man at least had foretold the future with accuracy: that old mole of a gravedigger Agnaar, who was now expected to bury Makan as he had said he would. And I was most unhappy to learn that my almost-father was to lie in a pauper's grave, in that desolate plot outside the walls where Gitte lay already. Instead of ordering a fine funeral for his jester, the King, it seemed, had washed his hands of Makan after the night of the banquet and left the matter to his chamberlain: a gloomy, chap-fallen pedant who had never succumbed to Makan's charm. He it was who declared that, since the fool had clearly drunk himself to death, he did not merit an honourable burial but should be interred close to Gitte. So on a bitter, cloud-shrouded morning, I and a few – a pitiful few – of the other servants gathered to bid farewell to Makan. No one of rank was present, save a priest who had come up from Helsingor to do his office. When it was over he hurried away, and I was reminded of the day Gitte was buried, when I had been angered by the hard words of the gravedigger. Though it was not Agnaar himself who did duty at the burial but his son Absalom, who in the years since had been made sexton.

Of course, Agnaar was there too: the rascal wouldn't have missed it for a bag of gold. White-haired and stoop-shouldered now, he declined to wield a spade, but stood near the mound of earth as he had done all those years ago, his eyes on me: the boy who had once insulted him, and was now a man. When it came time for his son to start work, the old rogue shuffled towards me.

'Save your sour breath,' I told him, 'for I'll not listen.'

'You should, boy,' Agnaar said, before turning aside; a great, yellow blob hit the ground as he spat. 'For I'm not here to gloat. We all come to dust, as will I soon enough - and Absalom will bury me, as likely he will you one day. Though whether it be here or in some fairer place shall depend on how you spend your years henceforth... or, is it of no concern to you, what she wished?'

For a moment I failed to understand him, then I realised he was speaking of my mother. Gitte, who had sworn at my birth that after death I would lie among people of rank. Had she spoken of this to Agnaar? I had no knowledge of it. Eyeing me from beneath tangled white brows, he sniffed and gave a nod.

'Think on it, Yorick. For if you reach my years, you'll know that the journey from womb to grave is but a flicker of light, a breath between nothing and eternity - and yet, how a man lives in that brief time shall decide how he goes to the afterworld.'

He looked towards his son, who was plying his spade with skill. In truth, nowadays I might give a snort of derision, having no time for his cod philosophy; but I was a younger Yorick then. Now the other servants – I cannot even call them mourners - were drifting away, some with nods in my direction. I began to move, but Agnaar gripped my arm fiercely.

'You think yourself above the likes of me?' He demanded. 'You who frolic for the King, and who'll take the place of his *hofnar* now he's gone?' Letting go of me, he gestured towards the grave. 'Well, hear this: you'll be hard put to fill his shoes, boy - remember that. Now go, and bid the better man farewell.'

And with a wave of his hand he sent me away, towards the diminishing pile of earth. Wordless now, I stood by the grave and watched Absalom do his work. Only when I turned to leave did he pause, leaning upon his spade in the exact same manner as his father, to watch me depart.

And *confiteo*: I shivered, as though a freezing wind had swirled about me.

Some days later I was called to attend my Lord. Or so I was told, and assuming this meant King Rorik I would have hastened at once to the presence chamber, until the messenger who summoned me corrected my error. He meant the new ruler of Jutland, he said: Horwendil, who had remained at Kronborg since the fateful banquet and as yet showed no sign of leaving - unlike his brother, the spurned suitor Feng, who had departed the following morning without ceremony. His Highness would receive me in the turret chamber, some distance from the High Hall, which he had taken as a station from which to order his affairs. So in some anticipation I made my way to the appointed place, was shown in by a liveried servant and made my bow - to find myself facing not merely Horwendil but also Gurutha, seated beside him wearing a splendid burgundy gown, over which was displayed the gold chain he had given her when they met. Graciously the Princess acknowledged my arrival, before turning to Horwendil, who did not. And his first words were:

'They say you're an even worse reprobate than Makan was, *Hofnar*. Do you mean to follow him in all you do, or have you a different path in mind?'

'In truth, Highness, all I know I learned from him,' I answered, somewhat sharply. 'I'm bound to serve my King however I can, and strive to lighten his cares as my father did...' whereupon on impulse I blurted: 'For he's King still, and commands me for whatever years remain to him.'

I swallowed; this was insolence, which I should have left unspoken. Rorik was indeed King of Denmark while he lived, despite seeing Horwendil elected his heir. Yet this man had power enough to harm me, or even have me cast out; and as to where I stood just now in Rorik's estimation, I had no notion. I'd not seen him since the feast, nor had any word from him. Berating myself silently, I awaited the response - but it was Gurutha who spoke.

'Loyalty does a man credit, Yorick,' she said sweetly. 'Hence, Lord Horwendil and I hope we may depend on you when we are crowned... then, I expect you've thought of that.'

'Of course, Highness.' I stifled a cough; there was much phlegm and coughing at Kronborg that winter. 'And my service to you is boundless, as always.'

'There – do you note his flattery?' With a rapid turn of her head, Gurutha faced her betrothed. 'Yorick has a slippery nature, which he can turn to use at the snap of a twig. What do you say – shall we take him with us to your seat, when we are married? Moreover,' she added, aware of the alarm her words caused me, 'do we then retain him as our fool when you are Denmark's King, and we return to Kronborg? The choice, of course, is yours.'

But it wasn't, and Yorick saw it.

He saw it when Horwendil's grim expression softened to a smile – more of a smirk, Makan would have said. And in that moment, I knew: the future king was besotted, and already in her power. Despite what had happened at the feast, when to all eyes it appeared the Princess had succumbed to Feng's brazen courtship, in a matter of days Gurutha had resolved to accept her father's decision and see what she could make of it. With that iron will of hers, that I knew only too well, she had forced Feng from her thoughts and bent her attentions to her husband-to-be. In time there would be a new King and Queen of all Denmark, but the King would be the lesser of the two, great warrior that he was; had not her father Rorik been a warrior too, only to be subdued by his brittle Queen whenever he returned? All this I saw, like a scroll rolled out before me - had the hex Edela, I wondered, seen what was to come in such a manner? These thoughts flew up so quickly, I was hard put to conceal my feelings. I stiffened, realising Horwendil was speaking.

'I think Yorick should remain here when we leave,' he said. 'Somehow, I doubt the duller clime of our court would suit his restless spirit. I see he's a man who moves swiftly, like a dancer...' he turned to his bride-to-be. 'Or do you wish it otherwise?' he asked. 'Whatever your desire, you know it shall be done.'

By the gods, thought Yorick, *the poor man's her lapdog already*; I could almost hear Makan snort with contempt. Was this how it would be – and was I to be Gurutha's hapless slave for the rest of my days? I drew breath, and awaited my fate.

'My desire…?' Gurutha raised her brows and appeared to ponder the matter. 'Why, my desire is yours, My Lord, and shall ever be. Yorick can stay and serve my father, as no doubt he prefers…' this with a sly look at me. 'Later, when we're come to our full estate, we might consider anew. Do you approve, Yorick?'

Approve? As if I had choice in the matter, relieved as I was. I bowed my thanks and waited to be dismissed, but Horwendil was not finished with me yet. Fixing me with a grim look, he said: 'We have observed your demeanour, *Hofnar*, as we have heard report of you. Your skills as a songster and a mime are beyond question, if somewhat indecorous to our tastes. You would be wise to curb your lewdness, and temper your behaviour to suit. When I am King here, I intend to make changes. Helsingor will be the heart of a new and bolder Denmark, known throughout Europe not merely for hospitality, but for manly courage, prowess and strength. Mark that, and strive to please.'

Upon which, having been dismissed with a curt nod, I got myself outside.

I went to the chamber: the old chamber, where both Gitte and Makan had expired. Apart from sleeping, my senses dulled by whatever strong drink I could beg or steal, I'd barely spent a moment there since finding my almost-father dead in his bed. The place was still strewn with his belongings: clothes, his old boots, his shawm in its leather bag. The last I would keep in memory of him, though I didn't play. One other thing I knew: I could not stay here. The room held ghosts that in time might come to trouble me – yet where could I go? The thought of a life under the rule of Horwendil and Gurutha filled me with dread, and wild notions began to spring to my mind. I might fly from Denmark and look for Eghil and Sveinn and the others. I might even go to Norway and seek out my mother's people, though I soon dismissed that as foolhardy. At last I came back to the thought that, for the present, I was in the hands of the ruler to whom I was yet bound: Makan's beloved King Rorik. I could perhaps beg an audience with him – but what if he refused to see me? What should I do then?

I rose and went from the room and from the castle, walking about in the cold until I was somehow drawn to the stables, where I had toiled under Asel; he was gone now, and a man I barely knew had his place. I was stepping inside, into the warmth and smells that sent years spinning away, when a shout stayed me. I looked round to find Trostann, whom I rarely saw in those days, crossing the yard towards me, and my heart lifted. My old friend – a rough-bearded farrier now - greeted me with a wry grin.

'Hail Yorick, royal fool,' he said, with a mocking bow. 'How do you?'

'Well enough – and you? Or should I first ask after your family?'

'Well enough,' he echoed, looking me over. 'And I'm glad I've seen you, if only to take farewell. We're to leave here soon – Ragnhild and me and the child – and go with Lord Horwendil, to serve him at his estate. The Princess advised it, so-'

'He obeyed,' I finished. 'Well, likely this will be a favourable turn for you...' I trailed off, my heart heavy on a sudden; everyone seemed to be leaving me. Seeing my expression, Trostann drew closer.

'It's what we want, Erik.'

At the use of my old name I started – and *confiteo:* I was near to tears. We eyed each other – but my feelings, I saw, were not his. There was a distance, a wariness that stopped short of disapproval, but only just. For a moment I was uneasy, wondering if Ragnhild had...

No, I dismissed it: she would not. I put out my hand and Trostann grasped it - a fierce grip, more used to handling hooves and fetlocks - but neither of us found the words. We stood for a while, then with a murmured farewell we parted. After which, numb with cold, I wandered back to the kitchens, to be greeted by Thura with her customary look of scorn.

'You're wanted,' she announced. 'The King's messenger was here – did you think folk have nothing better to do than look for you?'

'King Horwendil?' I muttered, my mind elsewhere. 'I saw him an hour since…'

'I mean King Rorik, clod,' Thura retorted. 'Are you drunk? You'd best get along – though if I were you, I'd wash my face first.'

A short while later, as clean and neat as he could make himself, Yorick entered the presence chamber and bowed low before his King. He straightened up, senses fully tuned to read the monarch's mood, and would have put on a smile save for the fact that Rorik wasn't looking at him. Instead he called to attendants who stood near, and with a gesture of dismissal ordered them away. Soon the two of us were alone, a rare and sobering experience for Yorick, who waited until the monarch turned his eyes upon him – to be taken aback by his words.

'What are they saying, out there?' Rorik demanded. 'Remember: speak truth to me, or I'll cut your tongue out myself.'

I flinched, gathered my wits and, for once, thought before I spoke.

'That Horwendil acts almost as if he's King of Denmark already. And the Princess as if she's Queen…' heart in mouth, I added: 'Then, she always did.'

There was a moment in which I thought I had angered him, but I should have known better; he held my gaze, then gave a nod.

'True enough.' A pause, then: 'Anything more?'

'That you spurned Makan because he insulted the Princess, and condemned him to a pauper's grave,' I blurted. 'He who was your most devoted servant.'

I looked down, regretting my words; in all likelihood, I thought, I had just contrived my doom. I stared at the floor, but when no answer came I lifted my head. Rorik considered for a moment, then took a drink from a chased cup that sat on a little table beside his throne.

'Now sing for me,' he ordered, wiping his mouth.

'Highness?' I blinked.

'Sing,' he repeated. 'The ballad of Hother, that so pleased my fawning guests - have you forgotten it?'

'No, I have not...' I swallowed, which the King took as a sign of thirst, whereupon he lifted the cup from his table again and held it out. In gratitude I took it and drank, tasting a deliciously sweet wine that was unfamiliar.

'It's Malmsey, from the far south – a land called Morea,' the King said as I returned the cup. 'Now, are you ready?'

I nodded, took a few breaths, and began the song of Hother. Not having thought on it since the night of the banquet I feared making a slip, but the words soon came. And when I saw Rorik close his eyes and sit back my voice swelled; I strove to move him, as I believed I had moved him that night. And in my mind's eye I saw Makan willing me on, his crinkled features stretched to a smile. I finished, drawing out the last note as before, then bowed. A silence followed before I looked up again, and was startled to see a tear rolling down the King's bearded cheek.

'So, Yorick...' With a sigh, he drew a broidered sleeve across his face. 'It seems it's just you and me now.'

I stared: it was an expression of friendship, to his new fool. So not knowing what else to do, I sought to lighten his mood. 'You and me,' I said, 'and a king-in-waiting who disapproves of me, and a brother who hates him, and a queen-in-waiting who can rule them both - what a household. If I were you, I'd shit myself.'

'Lucky you're not me, then,' Rorik grunted – whereupon he coughed: a harsh, grating sound from deep within his chest. Turning aside, he hawked and spat, before taking the cup of wine and draining it. By the time he'd turned to me again I was dismayed: he was ill, and making no effort to conceal it.

'Sire,' I began, 'should you not summon a physician...'

'I was angry with Makan,' he said, as if he hadn't heard me. 'But not because he insulted my daughter. I was angry because, as always, he dared to show me the folly of my ways

– and you're wrong to say I spurned him. I'll mourn him every day that's left to me... my dear, loving, loyal fool.'

In defiance, he fixed me with a look that would have quelled a regiment. 'As for his grave,' he went on, 'do you truly think he would want to be buried anywhere else but alongside Gitte?'

'I suppose not, Highness,' I admitted. 'I might have confused her wishes for me with what she wished for Makan...' and seeing the frown that appeared, I hurried on: 'She swore at my birth that I would lie in sacred ground, among the high-born - words spoken in pain and delirium, yet throughout my boyhood she would repeat them. Hence...'

I fell silent. Rorik's gaze was stern, though without anger.

'Do you think that's what Makan too would have wanted?' He demanded.

I gave a nod. 'He always tried to do his best for me.'

'Then it'll be done,' came the gruff reply. 'I'll order the chamberlain to have it written, that when Yorick dies he'll lie among the nobility. Are you content?'

'Indeed... I can but offer my heartfelt thanks,' I murmured.

'Is there anything else you want? You'd best ask now, while I'm in the humour.'

'My chamber...' I seized the moment. 'I cannot stay in the room where he died, both he and my mother.'

'The chamberlain will find you another. Is that all?'

Rorik coughed again, but this time controlled it. He dabbed at his watery eyes and waited, whereupon Yorick stiffened, then spoke as boldly – I should say as recklessly - as he dared. This could be his chance, he reasoned, to learn the truth: to free his mind from the suspicion that slept, but had never died. He paused, then tried to speak as levelly as he could.

'Forgive me, Highness,' I ventured, 'but there's one thing I must know. Before she died Gitte told me that you are... that you could be my true father. Of course, I didn't believe her, but she seemed to believe it was so... forgive me,' I repeated, before stopping my mouth. And in the silence that followed, I began to wonder if it was about to be stopped for ever – until there came a shout of laughter. I looked up quickly to see

Rorik's head thrown back, his jaws so wide I could see the gaps in his teeth: another revelation.

'I?' He shouted, struggling to rein himself. 'With the squinty one? By thunder, Yorick, I'd have had to be mighty soused to split the whisker with her, wouldn't you say?'

'Well... indeed, Highness,' I agreed quickly. 'Which is how she told it – of the drunken man who caught her that night, I mean. And, it was dark-'

'Dark?' Rorik let out another bellow of mirth. 'It would have needed to be black as pitch... your pardon, if I malign your mother,' he added, and dragged the sleeve across his face again. 'Yet there's no fathoming another's mind, who wishes thinking to make it so...' He breathed deeply, coughed again, and allowed his laughter to subside. Assuming a sadder face, he shook his head.

'No, Yorick - at risk of disappointing you, I'm not your father. Nor, I suspect, did Gitte truly believe it... folk will weave tapestries out of rags, if the urge is strong enough. That's a mystery I fear you will take to your grave. And mayhap it's best to think of him we both loved as your true father, is it not?'

'It is,' I answered, with a sigh. 'I'll honour his memory always, and strive to be the son he wanted...' I forced a cough. 'Speaking of splitting whiskers, there's much gossip about the Princess's wedding. Will it be soon, or... or will it not take place, after all?' I dared to ask, more in hope than anything else. 'That is, if your Highness has altered his mind?'

'I have not,' Rorik said firmly. 'A king doesn't go back on his word. The wedding shall take place here at Kronborg, in due time. Following that...' he looked aside. 'Following that, when I'm gone Denmark's future lies in the hands of others - mortal or otherwise,' he added, almost to himself. 'And you may bruit that among the gossips as you please.'

Upon which, thinking I was to be dismissed, I made my bow, but again Rorik stayed me. 'Now sing once more, before you leave me,' he said. 'There's that song Makan made, about the youth who encounters the *huldra* – do you recall it?'

To which Yorick, the King's Favoured Fool, smiled and nodded.

TWELVE

The wedding was in spring, of course: a sumptuous affair, if somewhat lacking in spirit. Kronborg was bright with blossom, and King Rorik had spent lavishly on food and entertainment. Though there were no players: since Eghil and the others had gone, the King appeared to have lost his appetite for interludes and the like – or so it was rumoured. What seemed more likely to Yorick was that, since Horwendil had little taste for such fare, Gurutha had chosen to humour him. A consort came from Helsingor to provide music for the wedding feast, and for the dancing and carousing that would follow into the night. Guests from across the realm attended, if fewer in number than those who had filled the castle for the great banquet at which Rorik had proposed his successor. Nor was Yorick called on to do more than sing and make a few jests – not of his best, I'll admit. And when night fell, and the wedded couple were escorted to their nuptial bed by a throng of young men, the business lacked its usual ribaldry. Having given his blessing to the union of Gurutha and her husband the King too retired, looking somewhat weary. Hence there was a palpable air of relief when the revellers returned to the High Hall, to fall upon the supper tables.

Yorick was among them, cup in hand, looking about for a likely maid to share his bed. In truth, though gratefully bestowed in my new, if somewhat cramped chamber under the roof at the northern end of the castle, I'd had few opportunities in recent months for serious rutting. Not that I was shunned: since replacing Makan as Favoured Fool and gaining the ear of the King, there were a number of maids willing to donate their favours. Even Bodil, the fair flower of the brewing-house, still unmarried, had hinted that she was willing to rekindle our brief liaison.

And yet such occasions were few; I was at Rorik's constant bidding, even if he seldom called me except to sing for him. To my eyes he had never truly recovered from the ague that troubled him through the winter. He was ageing fast, growing tetchier, falling at times into a melancholy from which I was hard put to rouse him. The best way, I discovered, was to talk bawdy to him, for which my store of crude jests culled from my stable-lad days came in most useful. The plain truth, however, is that when I diverted him with lurid tales of my latest conquests, they were just that: tales, fashioned from my own fancies. More than once, leaving him of a night-time to go to my bed, I fell to tugging my yard as though I were a green youth again, hot with thoughts of long-departed Dorethe, and of course of Ragnhild. But Ragnhild was gone with Trostann, to take up their places in Horwendil's castle in Jutland, ready for his return. Mulling on such matters, and in a somewhat poor humour, I was stood by the doors when I felt a tug on my sleeve, and turned to find myself facing Runa.

'Will you come with me?' She asked, in a low voice. 'I would speak with you.'

Well now: I lost no time in following her outside, until to my surprise she led me around the brewing-house, to the place where I'd once passed on gossip during my service as spy for Gurutha. And, as I was soon to learn, once again the Princess was the cause of our meeting, though in a way I could never have compassed. For no sooner were we out of sight of prying eyes than Runa turned abruptly and – I swear it - asked me to marry her!

'This is a jest,' I grunted. 'Who set you to it, and how much are they paying you?'

But quickly she shook her head. 'Listen, Yorick, for this chance may not arise again. The Princess will be leaving soon and I'm bound to go with her, which I'm loth to do. All that I know is here – my mother is not far away, and she grows old. Gurutha won't give me leave to visit her, so I might never see her again. More, Lord Horwendil looks grimly on me – I think he's jealous of my closeness to Gurutha. Once under his roof I know my life will be harsh – worse than it's been here. She's told me she'll never give me leave to depart... I'll be her body-servant to the end, at the mercy of her every whim till we both turn grey. My best hope is for a man who enjoys royal favour to speak to the King – to beg permission, for his own sake and for my loyal service, to take me as his wife. Then I could remain here...'

She paused, after what seemed one long, breathless burst, and – amazed as I was, standing there in the gloom - I would have spoken up, had she not hurried on.

'I know she'll return here to rule as Queen someday. But by then I'd be a settled wife - perhaps with children, and less appealing as a handmaid. Indeed, I'd do all I could to make myself disagreeable to her, so that she would bespeak someone younger – do you see? For I know no other way, Yorick, and that's the truth of it.'

She ceased talking, and *confiteo*: I was stunned. That this pretty young woman, who had once scorned me as a rake for whom she would never *spread her legs* – the memory sprang to mind, naturally – should wish to take me for her husband was beyond fancy. Yet she was in earnest, and she was afraid. I sensed desperation - something I'd never expected to find in Runa. My thoughts in a whirl, I was slow to find words, whereupon she spoke again.

'I know how your mind moves. You picture a constrained life, but it need not be so. I can be the wife you wish me to be: attentive, yet distant when it suits you. I couldn't change you, nor would I try. Though I'd be glad of children - it would delight my mother. There...' she let out a sigh. 'Will you think on what I've said – or might you even give an answer now? It would help me sleep, at the least, since the Princess is unlikely to call me before morning...' though I could barely see her, I glimpsed a rueful smile. 'So, Master Fool: I've blathered enough, and I'll-'

That was when I grabbed her and kissed her, almost yanking her off her feet. She stiffened at first, but after a while submitted and allowed me to press my mouth to hers. By the time I released her she was panting, and yet her arms had gone about my shoulders: a most promising development.

'By the gods, why didn't you ask sooner?' I blurted. 'Do you truly think I need to ponder it? I'd marry you at once, you...'

I stopped myself: it was a breeches-tightening moment, yet I held back. The Yorick of but a few months before would have taken her to his chamber and demanded we seal our betrothal forthwith, yet I knew this was not the time - or rather, Runa was not the maid for such. Instead I embraced her tenderly, feeling her go limp as she leaned against me, and soon there were tears. In sheer relief she wept, seeing at last an escape from a service which had become hellish to her. When I released her, holding her by the shoulders, she gave a great sigh.

'You have my thanks,' she breathed, with a shiver; the air was growing cool. 'And you'll have my body soon enough, despite what I once said to you. I ask nothing more, save one thing: that you'll never lie to me, as my mistress has done so often – as she does still, even to her own father. Will you swear it?'

'I will and I do,' I told her, moved to a tenderness I'd rarely known. 'And as for the matter of my appetites, you needn't fret. In my mind I've already bedded you more often than you may think…'

I broke off then, as her last words sank home: that Gurutha lied to her father. On a sudden, and despite the moment's portent, my instinct as loyal servant to Rorik was engaged, and with a frown I pressed Runa to speak further.

'I will, but not this night,' she answered. 'You know her character as well as I do…' she frowned suddenly. 'Yet now I fear the King may refuse you, when you beg leave to wed me,' she said. 'If Gurutha demands that he forbid it – you know how he grants her every wish…'

But I stayed her, putting a hand to her lips. 'Less so, nowadays,' I said. 'Indeed, to my mind he's grown weary of her. The betrothal to Horwendil was a sign of it, since she let her father understand she favoured his brother, and would sit beside him at the feast. Yet the King chose the duller man – not only for his steadfastness and loyalty, I believe, but to teach Gurutha a lesson. Pray don't torment yourself with this, but leave Rorik to me.'

'Well now…' In the gathering dark, her face softened. 'How you've grown, Master Yorick: a man who petitions the highest in Denmark.' She put out her hand, which I took, whereupon: 'That one was at the wedding, did you know?'

she murmured. 'He stood back, cloaked as if ready for a swift leave-taking. But he wouldn't miss it – she knew that, too.'

At first I failed to comprehend, then: 'You mean Lord Feng... he was here?'

'For a while, though not for the feast. He sent a message last night - to Gurutha, I mean. She said it was a farewell, that Feng wished her only happiness, and that he intended to travel on a pilgrimage to Rome, in hopes of being restored to his brother's favour one day. She made light of it, but she's not told her father, or Horwendil...' She shivered again. 'But let's not speak of them. You lift my heart – you may even heal it. I must go, but tonight I'll think of you. And after you've won an audience with the King, whenever it be...'

'It will be tomorrow, as soon as he's breakfasted,' I said, clasping her hand. 'And I'll not leave until he's granted what I ask, and what I wish with all my heart. Now, are you content?'

Whereupon we parted with another kiss, as sweet as any I'd known.

And that's as well; for it would be our last real kiss, ever.

See now, I come to another turnabout, as sad and fateful as any can be. The gods can be mean and fickle, twisting a man's hopes until he's close to madness. I believe now that this was what the hex Edela saw when she looked into my soul, and spared me a life of discontent by refusing to tell me my fate. Mayhap Gitte suspected as much, and tried to divert me in her clumsy fashion, with tales of the royal father who wasn't... but no matter. What transpired is known to the world, and when all's said and sifted, it came as small surprise to most.

So I'll tell of how, on the morning after the wedding of Horwendil and Gurutha, after carousing until dawn, all of Kronborg slept late except for Yorick. And of how Yorick presented himself at the door to his master's chamber, tipping a servant to go in and beg him for an audience on a matter of great import. And how the man soon emerged to send Yorick harshly away, and how there was then a great commotion, with attendants running and sentries hurrying to guard doors, and counsellors appearing half-undressed, and the King's old physician arriving at the bedchamber in his night-robe, and Yorick with a rising feeling of dread, loitering in passages... until at last, after hours had passed, he was called to the presence chamber where, among a throng of dismayed subjects, some weeping, he heard the words of the royal chamberlain, that made his heart stop.

King Rorik, son of Hother, had risen from his bed, called for a cup of malmsey, then ordered his body-servant to draw wide the curtains so that he might greet the day. Standing at his east window, bathed in sunlight, he had raised the goblet to his lips - whereupon the servant saw it fall to the floor and roll away, as the King too fell in a great, untidy heap. He did not speak, nor did he make a sound when he was lifted onto the bed where, almost two hours later, he died surrounded by counsellors and physicians, with his daughter Gurutha kneeling beside him. His face, they said, was serene when the end came; he merely closed his eyes and exhaled a final, rattling breath.

That same day, Horwendil was proclaimed King of Denmark and Gurutha his Queen, their coronation to follow after the proper period of mourning was passed. In the meantime, they would not leave Kronborg but remain there, to dwell in perpetuity.

And more: Gurutha announced that, on being crowned, she would take the name Gertrude, in honour of the saintly queen of that name, wife of the great Canute the Sixth of long-revered memory. And may the One True God, whom she now claimed to have worshipped all her days, watch over her, her husband and their future offspring for all time, she said.

As for her husband: the new King had decided, with her approval, to mark this change by taking the name Hamlet.

Confiteo: I'm spent now, with the mere telling of it.

THIRTEEN

Well now, pious Mattheus the chaplain has been here again, asking how goes my tale of repentance. If I could be troubled to rise from my pallet I would have kissed him, the sweet, gentle lamb. How he can serve a harpy like Queen Gertrude and yet preserve his innocence is beyond the understanding of a sinner like Yorick; then, do not men see what they wish to see? It goes well, I told him, and took occasion to ask him for more paper and ink, which he promised to supply. Mattheus' part in my tale should not be forgotten - but *satis*: a pox on me if I stray from my purpose, which is to tell all and be damned. *Legete* - that means 'read on' in Latin – while I speak of the reign of Gertrude and her husband.

The Bishop of Roskilde crowned them both, on a day of cloud and wind that some deemed inauspicious. But away with the doomsayers, let bells be rung and joy resound through the kingdom, announced the chamberlain - the new chamberlain, that is. The old dullard who'd served King Rorik was gone, and a younger man named Huginn had his place – chosen, everyone knew, not by the King but by his Queen, who liked the man's attentive manner. Nor was Huginn the only new arrival at Kronborg... and see now, I'm in such a muddle with recalling changes, I've called it by its old name. It was henceforth to be known as Helsingor, King Hamlet announced, after the settlement that lay under its mantle – a settlement which would grow, he said, to a great town. And yet, what would become clear was, it wasn't Helsingor which would grow to engulf the castle: rather, the castle would stretch out its arms to encompass the town. In truth it was to become a stout fortress, and the King its general: a commanding figure, often in armour, who would stride about the battlements as if prepared for assault at any time. And this was no idle fancy: the great sea rover saw Norway under Fortinbras as his natural enemy whom he planned to meet in battle soon, as he and his ancestors had fought the King's forebears... but forgive me, for again I leap ahead.

In truth the coronation, after the mourning for Rorik was over, proved neither joyless nor doom-laden; all thrones must pass on, and there was no denying that Hamlet was a proud and dignified King, if somewhat stiff and aloof by temperament. And despite her tiresome ways Gertrude was still Rorik's daughter: regal, and fair to look upon. Many expressed the sentiment, seeing her bedecked in her fine robes and gold chain, her crown fitting her as aptly as it should one born to rule. It was known by now that the new King doted on his wife, and would grant her every desire – one of which caused much gossip at Helsingor: Gertrude, it transpired, instead of sharing a bedchamber with her husband, would follow her mother in taking as her own the same great, tapestried room with gilt mirrors, where the former queen had died. And King Hamlet?

The King, for his part, was seemingly content with a nearby chamber, smaller and sparser which accorded with his tastes. For as Yorick had been quick to discern, this man was as much soldier as monarch, given to issuing orders with scant counsel from others. This might explain why Huginn was rarely seen in the presence chamber. It was more common to find the chamberlain in attendance on the Queen, which to Yorick's mind boded ill for some, including himself. His suspicions were confirmed when he was called one afternoon to face Gertrude alone - apart from Huginn, who stood nearby with his staff of office, a bemused smile upon his fleshy face. And I was uneasy to see the Queen occupying Rorik's old throne; a new one, similarly adorned, was set beside it for the King. Being Gertrude – use of her old name was now forbidden – she lost no time in coming to the nub of things.

'I've half a mind to have you cast out, Yorick,' was her opening volley. 'A fool's license is one thing, insolence bordering on treachery is quite another – and in our new elevation to Queen, tantamount to treason.'

So: once again, I awaited my doom. In truth I'd felt glum since the coronation, being stricken by the loss of my King, to whom I had gone to beg for Runa's hand in marriage on the very day of his death. Cruel fortune, that took him so abruptly and kept us apart: we'd had no chance to meet since, as

Gertrude now kept all her maids busy from morn until night. Moreover, she seemed to keep an especially close eye upon Runa, as if suspecting her of some mischief. And though I'd thought to ask my new King for the same favour, there had yet been no occasion: he had, it seemed, small need of a jester for his companion – or rather, his mind was bent to a different purpose, as I would soon discover.

'Treachery, Highness?' I repeated, putting on a bewildered look. 'I don't understand what you-'

'Stop!'

It was Gurutha's voice: the wilful girl whose cries once put fear into the hearts of all within earshot; now that she was Queen Gertrude, why should it be different? In show of humility, I bowed my head.

'Runa,' the Queen said. And when I looked up sharply: 'Did you truly dare to ask her to be your wife?'

'I did, Highness,' I answered, swallowing and making a swift recovery; this was no time to inform her that it was Runa who'd done the asking. 'Your pardon, but it's my heart's desire – I would have begged leave from King Rorik, had he...' I broke off, as her expression sent my spirits plummeting.

'It's my leave you should have sought,' Gertrude snapped. 'But then, you knew I would refuse. My women are not for the likes of you – have you forgotten my words to you, long ago? No, you have not – so knowing my mind, you went behind me to my father. Well, he's gone and his ways are gone with him. You will, of course, forgo any hopes of taking Runa to wife – as you may forget the easy life you've enjoyed as Favoured Fool. The King has no need of your rhymes - indeed, it may be that he has no need for you at all. We await his pleasure.' She paused, enjoying my plight, whereupon the chamberlain chose his moment to speak.

'Highness, might I...?' Huginn cleared his throat, somewhat affectedly to my ears, and having gained Gertrude's attention: 'I understand the King has some service in mind for Master Yorick after all,' he said in a mild voice (*confiteo:* how many times since have I wanted to mash his smiling features to a pudding?). 'When he dines tonight with his captains, in gratitude for their loyalty, he's made it known he will have the *hofnar* attend him. Beyond that I know little, save-'

'When was this?' The Queen's icy voice cut him short; how much the poor man had yet to learn, thought I. 'And why was I not told?'

Huginn blinked. 'Forgive me, Highness... I only learned of it a short time ago. Likely the King meant not to trouble you with such a trifle.'

'I'll decide what's trifling,' Gertrude retorted, and seeing her grip the arms of the throne tightly, both chamberlain and jester stiffened. 'And in the future, never fail to inform me of anything my husband says when I'm not present, or...'

She stopped and threw a swift glance at me - and you could have pushed Yorick over with a finger. The years fell away, and he was the dumbstruck youth who was ordered to be the Princess's eyes and ears at Court. Now Huginn was to have that honour; I might have pitied the man, had I not already decided to dislike him. But I read the warning in her eyes, and knew I must keep such knowledge hidden. A short silence followed, in which the chamberlain resorted to more throat-clearing.

'Of course, Highness, I was remiss...' his gaze strayed towards me. 'I believe it's no more than a matter of some rough entertainment, suited to a soldiers' mess – the King must play the manly host, when he wishes to bind his men together for war. I myself was not summoned, and yet if it please you...'

'It does,' Gertrude said at once. 'It was careless of him not to invite you – you may tell him it's my wish that you attend, along with Yorick.'

To which Huginn bowed, and that appeared to be the end of the matter. For Yorick, sick at heart at having to abandon all hope of wedding Runa, dismissal could not come soon enough; even the prospect of entertaining the new King, and perhaps winning favour, could not restore his spirits. In misery he stood while Gertrude seemed to gather her thoughts – then:

'The King is in the throes of settling affairs left in disarray by my father,' she said, sitting more erect. 'One order, to our surprise, was to Lord Huginn's predecessor concerning the matter of your burial, Yorick.' Seeing me give a start, she put on one of her half-smiles; some habits neither man nor woman can change. Having let the thought strike home, she delivered her parting volley.

'It's a matter of great sadness to us, that King Rorik's noble mind was somewhat dulled towards the end,' Gertrude said. 'What put such a notion into his head is a mystery - but you must know that the order is rescinded, as in all propriety it should be. There's no prospect of your being laid to rest among the tombs of our forebears, however long you may live. I pray you'll take that thought away – and more, that you heed the King's words to you when we last spoke, about tempering your behaviour. Helsingor is to be a godly place, of rightness and humility. Now leave us.'

Which I did, so readily that I almost forgot to make my bow. As I bent low, I found myself gazing at the Queen's shoes, which were of the same red leather as those she'd worn as a girl, if more finely crafted. That was the picture I took away as I got myself outside to the passage, where I slumped upon a bench.

So, when I'm dead I'll lie with my almost-father and my mother, thought Yorick; that's no bad thing, even if it was not Gitte's desire. In truth, I found that I cared little. And yet here was another turning, onto a path that was yet hidden. Had I known it was the beginning of my fall, I might have fled from Helsingor then; but I had work to do yet, and was ready to do it.

That night the High Hall was filled once again, but not with chattering knights and ladies as in Rorik's time. Huginn had spoken aright: the entire company consisted of men, from marshals of the field to lowly ensigns – the head and backbone of King Hamlet's army, now strengthened by others newly arrived from his lands in the west. Their talk was loud and ribald, but of a different stamp to that I had grown used to: tempered with harshness, even cruelty. And soon after making my entry, I would learn the measure of it.

'*Hofnar* – Master Yorick!' The King beckoned me forward to stand before the High Table. 'I had almost forgot - are you ready to entertain us? The song of Hother perhaps, which once delighted us... or then again, perhaps not.'

Cup in hand, he levelled a gaze at me which I could not fathom - but then, I barely knew him; indeed, it would be years before I began to do so, and to revise my first opinions. What I saw then was a different man from the attentive spouse who had sat beside Gertrude that day, eying me with disapproval: here, seated among his officers, was one at ease with himself. I bowed and awaited his pleasure, while the talk about me died down. Soon the eyes of most were turned in my direction, whereupon the man seated beside the King, a ruddy-faced commander with scars, spoke up.

'Tumbler, are you?' he barked. 'Well sport yourself, and let's gauge your mettle.'

I shifted my gaze, to find myself staring at the bottom of the man's cup as he quaffed. It struck me that many of the company were already enlivened by drink, despite the earliness of the hour. Summoning a smile, I faced the King again. 'What will you have, Highness?' I asked. 'A song, a rhyme, or some other fare? It's both my duty and desire to please you, as it was my King... I mean, as it was-'

I stopped, cursing my clumsiness. King Hamlet disliked any mention of his predecessor, who was loved and mourned at Helsingor, and indeed throughout all of Denmark. And I was yet to learn how much the man burned to prove his worth, meaning to do it through conquest and the crushing of his enemies. Swiftly I sought for a means of turning the matter about, of doing the unexpected - but it was too late.

'By thunder, what insolence!'

It was the ruddy-faced marshal who spoke, eying me over his cup with a look of outrage. And before I could speak, he picked up a chicken leg from his platter and hurled it, hitting me squarely on the nose.

The silence that fell was immediate, and filled with expectation: what, they wondered to a man, would I do - and more, what would the King do? Eyes went from the jester, standing rigid with the remains of a smile on his features, to Hamlet... and in that moment, Yorick saw his fate was sealed.

'A passable hit, sir,' the King allowed, with a nod to his companion. 'But I'll match it.' With that, he took up a half-eaten barley loaf and threw it, catching me on the brow.

I flinched - and Makan's voice flew to mind: I saw him in the orchard, squashing the apple on his nose, telling me to seize the bully's power and turn it to my own use. At once I stooped, picked up the bread and placed it atop my head.

'My thanks, Highness,' I said, grinning. 'I was in sore need of a new bonnet.'

Alas, nobody laughed.

There was but a moment, before a second loaf sailed across the hall from somewhere and struck me on the neck. No sooner had I turned than another missile hit me from closer by – and it being a pear, that hurt. I was on the point of grabbing it, having a notion to bite into it and, Makan-fashion, pronounce it too sour, when something softer landed on my shoulder: a hunk of pork, with a wad of fat attached. In growing alarm I straightened, knowing what was afoot - and as if at a signal, missiles of all kinds began to fly at me, from scraps of food to balled-up napkins and even a silver goblet, which fortunately missed. And throughout the bombardment I racked myself for some way to respond: should I retaliate, or submit like a pilloried felon and take my punishment?

For punishment it was: I knew it when, wheeling and ducking as best I could, I glanced at the King, and saw - what? Amusement, or satisfaction? Not displeasure, despite his once using the word *indecorous* to me – and how indecorous was this? The pelting, now accompanied by laughter and shouts, was grown intolerable; men stood up, taking aim at their victim, hooting at those who missed. Soon I was not merely besmeared: I was bruised, angry and shamed, but forced to conceal it – was this, I wondered, what Makan had warned me about? In vain I looked again to the King, who refused to meet my eye: clearly the high spirits of his men were of greater importance than the plight of his jester. And the longer this went on, I knew, the harder it would be for me to bear it – but if I tried to leave the hall would I be made to return, to face an even worse penalty? Seeing no other remedy, I was on the point of falling into a swoon, pretending worse injury than I had - my player's days were not so far behind that I couldn't fake it – when matters took a different turn. Cowering as I was, trying to cover head and face, it took a moment for me to realise the pelting had ceased, whereupon in relief I straightened and looked to the High Table – to see the King on his feet, hands raised as he called for order.

'Enough - shame on you all!' He cried – which produced merely a chorus of laughter; in dismay, I saw the look on his face and knew it was not one of censure. Nor did it show any sympathy for his hapless fool, who cut a sorry figure: besmirched, panting - and beaten. No matter that it was a cruel victory against a defenceless foe, if foe he was: winning was all to these men, who would brook nothing less. Grimly Yorick eyed his monarch, until:

'On the table, *Hofnar*, if you please,' the King ordered, before turning to the companions on his right. 'You, sirs – make space for him.'

It was done at once: a sweeping away of dishes and platters to leave a clearing in the centre of the table. Whereupon real fear arose in my heart: what further ordeal had they in mind for me? I might have turned tail and ran, save that the doors were closed and attendants posted. Instead I found myself seized by the arms and propelled towards the table, where a stool was placed for me to clamber up. There was no choice: willing hands gripped me, helping me onto my platform. There I stood, the easiest target a man could make – and only then did I notice Huginn.

He had been sitting some distance from the King, near the end of the table. Now that seats were vacant, their occupants having risen to watch the sport, he stood up and made his way to Hamlet's side. I saw him speak in the King's ear, saw the look of annoyance that followed, and the glance thrown in my direction. Hardly daring to hope, I kept my eyes on both of them as the mob swirled about me, laughing and bawling, faces flushed with wine and anticipation. Some had missiles ready, which from such close quarters spelled even worse disaster for me – yet they held back as if waiting for the command. When it came it was a disappointment to them - but salvation for Yorick.

'Loyal followers, worthy marksmen - I pray you, cease!'

Still on his feet, Hamlet called them to order with an indulgent smile, waving away voices of protest which arose. One drunkard ignored him and made to throw a crust at me, but was stayed by his friends. The noise diminished, men quieting their fellows, until the King spoke up again.

'You're most fortunate, *Hofnar*,' he announced, with a look in my direction. 'Our chamberlain begs mercy for you, and we will indulge him. We'd thought to make some example of you – to show that brazen insolence, of the kind you were wont to employ in your service to the late King Rorik, will not be brooked in our court.'

He paused, then waved a hand in dismissal. 'Now leave us. You may remain at Helsingor for the present, while we decide how to make use of you – or indeed, whether you have any use... Lord Huginn?'

He turned to the chamberlain who murmured something, then nodded in my direction. I needed no bidding, but scrambled down from the table and forced my way through the disappointed revellers, receiving a few kicks and gibes in the process. After bowing to the King, I was on the point of making my escape when I saw Huginn signal me to wait. Whereupon, in mingled relief and confusion, I stood near the doors while he made his way unhurriedly towards me. The company, meanwhile, lost interest and returned to their feasting.

'A word with you, Master Yorick.'

He nodded to an attendant, who opened one of the doors and stood by it. Whereupon, to my discomfort, Huginn placed an arm about my bespattered shoulders and pressed me to him, turning me as rigid as his staff of office.

'The King may have small need for you, henceforth,' he murmured, bending close. 'Yet for the Queen and for myself, the case could be otherwise.'

He paused to let me digest his words. I was in his debt for having rescued me from further assault, and he was keen to ensure that I knew it.

'Stay out of sight and out of trouble, would be my advice,' he continued, in a fatherly voice. 'As for your unbridled cavorting with servants of the other sex, I'd counsel discretion there too... if you must indulge, do it in secret. In time you may be called to some service befitting your skills - are you content?'

Well, a pox and a plague on the malt-worm - was I content? Yet what else was I to do, but show gratitude? Strike me dead if I fail, and let me kiss your arse, sire, you're a true nobleman and no mistake. Or some such. In truth I don't remember what I answered. Let it be said that I agreed until he released me from his grip, then got myself outside with a nimbleness Makan would have been proud of. Shame and derision upon me: let me lay aside my pen and drink to take away the taste.

And yet to my surprise, some weeks later I would spend a brief moment with Runa; I drink to that too - to the joy and even the sadness of it.

FOURTEEN

It was late evening, on a summer night of balmy fragrance, when I stepped outdoors to dampen my gloom with a cup of wine lifted from the kitchen. Scarcely noticing where I walked, I soon found myself behind the brewing-house where I used to meet Runa in happier times; would that I'd relished them while I could. For what was Yorick now, but a bag of memories? A thing of air, wandering about Helsingor unneeded and unheeded? *Confiteo:* I believed then that the wave of fortune which had borne me, had carried me forward from ragged stable-lad to Favoured Fool – the luck that Gitte had spoken of - had ebbed at last.

And it was about this time that the *mareridt* began to visit me.

It started soon after my night of humiliation, when I had been harshly used by the King's men in the High Hall. Angry and shamed, and not a little nervous of what Huginn might want from me, I took to my chamber for days, sleeping only fitfully. Waking once in pitch darkness, I was thrown into a cold fear: there was a great weight on my chest, pinning me to the pallet. More, there was an odour which I knew only too well: the smell of horse. I even fancied I heard the breathing of the mare - felt it on my face, though I could see nothing. Rigid with terror, unable even to cry out, I lay damp with sweat – until Makan's voice came out of the dark.

'You disappoint me, Erik,' he said. 'You forget what I taught you, and do only the expected.'

I coughed, my mouth dry as parchment. Like a manikin I lay there, struggling to turn my head from the mare's breath; I could neither move nor speak.

'You lost the battle even before it was joined,' Makan accused. 'You should have seized the moment – returned what was thrown at you, with greater vigour. Men of war respect a man who fights back, but scorn a coward.'

But that's not what you taught me! I wanted to shout. *As when you crushed the apple on your nose, I thought to make them laugh...* but I was dumbstruck.

'Heed me, and remember,' came his voice again. 'Chance may yet come...'

He grew fainter; I was desperate to speak to him, but words caught in my throat. And still the mare sat, an immoveable weight that drove the air from my lungs - I believed I would suffocate. I tried to struggle, but my limbs were leaden. Terror overcame me - whereupon I awoke shouting, my arms flailing about as though I were possessed.

The *mareridt* had been; and only now did I understand Makan's gloom, when he'd stared into the fire that day and told me of it.

It came again after that, perhaps three or four times, each as frightening as the last. I cannot well recall the dreams now; I only know Makan never returned, nor did Gitte come. And it saddened Yorick, who began to lose his jollity and hence his very purpose - what use is a jester who cannot jest? Not that he was called upon to do so, nor even to sing; having no other choice, he was obliged to follow Huginn's advice and stay out of sight as best he could.

Once again, I began to harbour thoughts of flying from Helsingor and taking my chances in the world beyond, or of seeking out Eghil and the others. *Confiteo*: I shed tears thinking of the time I'd spent with them, even playing the simpering maidservant in *The Jealous Husband* – which made me think of the night that followed, when I first tasted the delights of womankind with Ragnhild. But *satis*: let the memory of what happened in the brewing-house return me now to that summer's night when I sat outside with my back to its wall, slurping stolen wine. For in truth I was loth to go to my bed, as I had often been since the *mareridt* began to visit me. I was mulling over my piteous state when there came a voice that startled me so, I almost believed I dreamed – but it was Runa.

'Yorick... at last.'

She rounded the wall so suddenly that I jumped to my feet, dropping my cup – but before I could speak, she placed her hand over my mouth.

'Soft – I've little time. I came here before, but never found you. You've become invisible… some even said you'd gone away, but I didn't believe them.'

She took her hand away then, and thinking to kiss her I leaned close, but to my dismay she drew back and shook her head. 'It's no use, Yorick… you must put aside those thoughts. My ways are trammelled – as I suspect yours are too.'

'Come away with me – come now,' I said, finding my voice along with remained of my spirits. 'You can run… I've seen you run. I'll find a way out of the castle - we could go down to the Sund, and beg one of the fishers to take us across. I've a few *pennings* in my purse… or we can go south-'

'Yorick, no.' She would have stopped my mouth again, had I not caught her hand. 'I can't. My mother grows feeble - and besides, she has me watched.'

'Your mother does?' I muttered. 'How can that be-'

'Gurutha!' Came her impatient answer. 'Or Gertrude, as she is now…' she drew a breath. 'She won't forgive me for wanting to marry you - and I should beg your forgiveness for revealing it. She knows me too well… she saw my mind was elsewhere, and wormed it out of me. I could never deceive her for long-'

It was my turn to stop her, pressing fingers to her lips. I believed she would weep, but no tears came. She was changed, I saw with a sinking heart: a prisoner who sees no means of escape. But she grasped my hand and held it.

'You could go – and you should,' she said. 'What is there to stay here for?'

'There's you,' I answered, but the words only pained her.

'I told you, put away such notions. There is a doom settling over Helsingor - do you not feel it? We in Gertrude's service do, with each day that passes – yet we must hide our thoughts, and appear content. Moreover, we must confess our sins now, or risk her displeasure.'

'Confess to whom?' I demanded. 'And what wrong have you ever done?'

'To Gertrude's new chaplain, Mattheus,' Runa answered. 'Have you not seen him? Young and handsome... he could have the pick of the maids if he chose, save that he's sworn to self-denial.' She put on a wry look. 'Not the kind of man for you, Yorick.'

I thought for a moment, recalling that I'd seen a stranger going into the chapel of late, but had barely given him a thought. Now my unease grew: what kind of realm did Gertrude and her husband mean to fashion? I wondered. Were laughter and gaiety, carousing and even romance to be banished? On impulse I told Runa what had happened to me at the King's feast, which troubled her.

'You should be wary of Lord Huginn,' she said. 'He and Gertrude are close – I believe it was at his urging that she took Mattheus into her service. And whatever he has in mind for you, I fear it bodes ill.'

'I keep out of his way,' I told her. 'As you said, I've become invisible.'

She gave a sigh, squeezing my hand. 'I must go - don't try to stay me. Likely my absence has been noted already.' She turned, then checked herself:

'There's a secret I'll tell before we part,' she said, 'which may be of use to you, though I'm unsure how.' She spoke as if afraid of being overheard, though we were alone. 'The Lord Feng has returned to Denmark and stays nearby, in hiding.'

I blinked and would have spoken, only for her to cut me short.

'That isn't all: I believe Gertrude's met with him. She rides out sometimes, while the King's away viewing his fortresses...' She paused. 'Swear you'll never reveal who told you this, Yorick – I beg.'

'I swear,' I said. 'Nor shall you beg...' I frowned as the import of her news struck me. 'Has she truly grown so reckless?' I asked. 'Or merely so brazen, she doesn't fear the King?'

'She thinks him pliant, so she can mould him to her will,' Runa said. 'Do you know what she calls him behind his back?

"Amlodi", after the simpleton in the sagas. Dress my hair well, so I may look my best for old Amlodi, she orders. She has no love for him, Yorick, but mocks him for a dull-witted soldier.' She fell silent – then delivered tidings that rendered me speechless.

'And hence, he won't suspect he may not be the father of her child.'

I froze, and seeing my expression she gave a nod. 'The news is yet to be announced, but her maids know. She hasn't bled her courses in weeks.' She paused again, then: 'It may come to naught - her mother lost children before she them carried to term. And if the King isn't the father, that would be the best outcome. For she rarely beds him – have you not heard?'

I shook my head. In truth I hadn't listened to gossip for weeks – and no-one, it seemed, troubled to tell me anything. 'What treachery has been done,' I said at last. 'This could spell ruin... if not for the Queen, then for the kingdom. I pity us – I pity all of Rorik's people.'

'We're no longer his people,' Runa said, most forlornly. And with a quick, darting movement she kissed me on the cheek, breathed farewell and left me.

Well now: what months were those that followed, upon the announcement of the Queen's pregnancy. Bells were rung, messengers despatched to every part of the kingdom and midwives hired - and yet while Gertrude's child grew in the womb, Yorick seemed to wither.

From being near-invisible, I had become a shadow: prowling in corridors or hiding in my chamber, half-expecting a knock which meant the King's servants were come to throw me out. I confess I grew shabby, rarely troubling myself about my appearance. I drank more, when I could get it, but ate less. I slept less too, even though the *mareridt* didn't often visit: my own restlessness woke me, driving me to pace about the room, knocking my head on its beams in the dark. Sometimes I ventured outdoors, pleading a sick stomach to the sentries who challenged me. I would walk in the garden or even to the stable-yard, without waking the boys who doubtless slept soundly in the hayloft. Once I went as far as the door to the Sund path, where Gitte had once led me, but it was now nailed up and impassable. By dawn, weary and wet with dew, I would be back in the chamber to fall on my pallet. There I would lie until late in the afternoon, before slouching to the kitchens to beg a supper.

Such a wretched life could not continue; I knew it well enough, though I had neither the means nor the will to change it. Until, with the nights closing in again and winds coming up from the Sund, there came a day that brought – not salvation, not for Yorick, but a change at least. And so low was he, that any shift in his fortunes just then was a meal to a starving man.

It was near dusk, and I was idling in the kitchen garden when someone called me. Looking about, I saw one of the stablemen walking towards me, a man whose name I did not recall. I awaited him, noting the look of disdain on his face, whereupon his words startled me.

'You're to come to the stables for your horse,' he announced.

'My horse?' I shook my head. 'You're mistaken, friend, for I have none.'

'I'm not your friend, *Hofnar*,' the fellow retorted. 'And I don't mistake. You're wanted, and I've done my part bringing the order. Obey or not, it's your affair.'

He strode off leaving me nonplussed; yet, what should I do but obey, if for no other cause than curiosity? Following his retreating back, I made my way to the stable yard where a brazier burned in the gathering gloom, to find a stout figure standing beside it, warming his hands. Mighty curious, I approached him - and recognised the Lord Huginn.

'Yorick...' In the firelight he looked me over, making no effort to hide his distaste. 'You are a most ragged and displeasing sight.'

I made a clumsy bow and straightened up, to the sound of hooves: a small but sturdy Friesian gelding was being led out of the stable doors, bridled and saddled. Drawing it was the man who had summoned me from the kitchen garden. Having delivered the reins to Huginn, he went back inside.

'Shall we take a turn about the courtyard?' The chamberlain said. 'You may lead him – his name is Kappi. You haven't forgotten how to handle horses, I assume?'

In bewilderment I took the rein from him, half-suspecting this was some kind of jest. But I moved close to Kappi, putting a hand on his neck and murmuring a few words; he was unafraid, and seemed of a gentle enough nature. At my tug on the rein he started forward, and the two of us followed Huginn under the archway and round the wall to the main courtyard, where we halted. Torches burned in iron stands, their flames wild in the breeze. On the battlements, in silhouette, sentries stood at their posts.

'He's yours,' the chamberlain said, with a nod towards Kappi. 'A gift from the Queen... a most generous one, to my mind.'

I started - and recalled the night he'd rescued me from the High Hall, put his arm about me and told me he might have a use for me; so now, thought I, the debt is about to be called in. Yet my instinct, naturally enough, was to feign ignorance.

'I don't understand, my lord,' I murmured. 'How have I earned such favour?'

'Well, in truth you haven't,' came the reply. 'Not yet.'

Huginn lifted his head, drawing long breaths as the wind ruffled the fur collar of his gown. Then he turned and indicated that we should stroll the courtyard: two men having a leisurely conversation before retiring for the night. Drawing Kappi behind, I walked beside him.

'You know of course that the Queen is *enceinte*, as the Franks would have it,' he resumed. 'Hence, her physicians insist it's unwise for her to ride... a disappointment to Her Highness, who delights in viewing her domain.'

Yorick waited.

'She's spoken of you with some sadness, of late,' the chamberlain went on. 'How you seem to have displeased the King, who no longer desires you at Court. Some of her councillors say you should be put to other kinds of work, or even dismissed from service... I, however, am not among them.'

Still I waited.

'The Queen has honoured me by taking me into her confidence,' Huginn said, looking straight ahead. 'She would remind you of the special bond of trust you and she enjoy, Yorick. A closeness most rare between a monarch and a serf... yet your loyalty, she assures me, is boundless. I hope you'll never give me reason to doubt that.'

This was no statement, but a question. On realising it, I summoned a respectful look. 'No reason at all, sir, that I can compass... I would swear it on my life.'

'That's most wise.' The chamberlain had tucked his hands into his wide sleeves, and was walking as stately as a bishop. 'For your life would indeed be forfeit - in a most unpleasant manner, too - should you fail in the service the Queen has bespoken for you. A service to be performed in private, I should add, with precision and with complete discretion.'

I swallowed; my mouth was dry, as it often was in those days. I would have given a good deal for a mug of ale. My mind leaped back to that dusty room, years before, when the young Princess had trapped me and demanded I pleasure her... then to the High Hall when I sang the Song of Hother, and caught her eye as she sat smiling beside her suitor...

'What kind of service would that be, sir?' I ventured.

'It's nothing, beyond taking the role of a messenger,' came the casual reply. 'You were a player once, I understand... a trifling matter, for one of your skills.'

So that's why I need a horse, thought I; the notion of Gertrude lavishing such a gift upon me without good reason was, of course, utterly foolish. The import of the matter began to dawn on me, whereupon:

'You will start tonight,' the chamberlain said. 'Here's the letter...' he dug in his gown and produced a sealed packet. 'Guard it well, and place it in no other hands than those of the man to whom it's addressed.'

I gazed at him. 'Tonight? But it grows dark... and I haven't been astride a horse in years. I might fall, or-'

'I'd advise you not to,' Huginn broke in. 'The message must be delivered by morning. If you lose your way you can wait by the road until dawn, then make haste. The horse has been fed - it's but a matter of ten leagues or less.' He threw me a disapproving look. 'It's a pity there's no time for you to change your attire. You should remedy that when you return, and improve your appearance – the Queen instructed me to give you this for such purposes.'

A purse appeared, its contents jingling; in spite of my misgivings I took it, along with the package.

'But I cannot read,' I mumbled. 'Hence, how am I to know who it's for?'

'You'll know him, I think,' the chamberlain said. 'As he will know you.'

He paused, then: 'As for your destination, it's somewhat remote, but I trust a man of your resources will find it. The farm is called *Saltfelter*. You take the west road as far as the *jagthytte* – King Rorik's old hunting lodge. There's a tiny village beyond that, where you'll cross a stream to your left. You then follow a path through the forest until you emerge in open fields... *Saltfelter* is beyond. You may get a breakfast if you're lucky, but you'll say nothing to the people there, beyond what is necessary. As soon as the horse is rested you will return here. Your silence thereafter will be taken as a sign that the message was safely delivered – though if there's a reply, you will bring it at once to me. Is that plain enough?'

In silence, I nodded.

'Good... now, the gates are still open. You should hurry before they close for the night.'

Huginn shivered, pulled his tippet about his shoulders and walked off. I watched him disappear, then turned to Kappi and, with my senses still reeling, placed a foot in the stirrup.

'I hope you and I will be friends,' I said as I grasped the pommel. 'For you need only fall into a ditch, and my life's as good as over. So - shall we set forth?'

And by the gods, I swear the horse not only nodded but winked, as if to say: *your life and likely mine too, Yorick. You'd best not fail either – is that plain enough*?

FIFTEEN

Even now, warm and comfortable as I am, I'm inclined to shiver when I recall that ride in the dark, let alone what came after.

Not that there was danger: the road was clear, there having been little rain of late, and the moon's light was enough to see by. And in truth, as I began to settle into my journey, feeling the rhythm of the horse's gait, my spirits lifted despite the circumstances - for by now I'd guessed who the message was for. The weight of the commission lay heavy upon me, and yet, when I turned it about, I saw why Gertrude – doubtless with Huginn's connivance – had chosen me as her courier. For who but Yorick was so in her power, that he would spare no effort to obey her? Who else lived under sentence of death, were she to carry out her old threat of accusing him of fumbling her as a girl? The King, I knew, would not doubt her, and his justice would be swift and terrible. Hence, by bizarre turn of fate, I was now caught up in the Queen's private business: her secret liaison with his brother.

It had to be so: clever Runa, who saw more clearly than anyone I knew, was wise to the matter. Gertrude, who never failed to place her own desires above all else, had succumbed to Lord Feng's advances from the start – from the very day they met, when he'd wooed her so shamelessly before Rorik and his entire Court. And it seemed to me now that her marriage was but a sham: a cloak beneath which she could pursue her own ends. The Queen rarely bedded her husband, Runa had said - which is small surprise, thought I, if she were meeting her lover and sating her lust with him. Her brazenness sobered me – Yorick, who regarded almost any woman as his prey. That Feng too could be so reckless, risking all in cuckolding his brother's wife, shook me even more - was he besotted with her, as was King Hamlet? I doubted it: I had seen the man's demeanour that day he came to Rorik's court in expectation of winning the Princess, as I'd watched him at the feast and seen how he charmed her, delighting her with his attention.

Yet, I asked myself, when all was said and sifted, what profit could there be in his bedding her behind his brother's back? Aside from the risks, the closer the two of them grew the more bitter would be their parting – for a parting had to come, at some later time. And now that the Queen was pregnant, what chance would they have to be together? Was that the substance of the message I carried, I wondered: that they must break off their affair for a while – even for ever? Though it seemed unlikely to Yorick that Gertrude would gift him a horse for a single journey – which thought chilled him further: on a sudden, the grim prospect arose of his becoming a regular messenger between the Queen and her lover.

What pious Mattheus would think of it all, I cannot imagine.

Throughout my ride I mulled over the matter. The night was cold and I was poorly clad for travelling, something that had troubled Huginn not a jot. The packet was tucked inside my jerkin, the purse tied to my belt; I'd stopped on the road to make them safe. Thereafter I made what speed I could, alternately trotting and walking the horse through that windy night; I would not risk a canter for fear of mishap. Though Kappi was a good mount: I knew it within the first hour, as I began to know his gait and manner. And then, after another hour had passed and Helsingor lay far behind, a notion sprang up with such force that I drew rein and halted. There in the saddle, with the horse's breath clouding in the dim light, I recalled Runa's words at our last meeting: *You could go... what is there to stay for?*

It was true; and never before, I realised, had I been provided with the means to carry it out. I had a horse and a full purse - moreover I had my wits. I could seek out Eghil and the players – failing that, I had enough skills to turn my hand to some other trade than fooling. I could be free of the King and Queen – a pox on them, and on Huginn and everyone else. There was Runa, of course; I was torn by the thought of not seeing her again. But she would understand – it was she who'd urged me to fly. Why then did I hesitate?

Confiteo: I've written it before, and I write it again: Yorick is and was a great coward, whose fear of the consequences of abandoning his mission overrode his desire to escape. For such a failure, of course, would neither be borne nor forgiven: Gertrude's rage would follow me wherever I went, in the form of armed pursuers under orders not to return without the wretched fugitive in chains. I could imagine the charges: theft of a horse and a purse, both crimes punishable by death... numb with cold, I faced the bleak truth: that I had no choice but to go on.

So with heavy heart I shook the reins and rode, stopping to rest a while later, though too cold to sleep. By dawn I had reached the ruined hunting lodge, where there was a water-trough. Thereafter, both horse and rider having satisfied their thirst, I followed Huginn's directions easily enough, passing through a poor village where smoke was beginning to rise from the huts, and finding the stream as he had said. Kappi clattered over a bridge onto a rising path, with woodland ahead. In the forest I urged him to greater speed: the place was dark and wild, a likely cover for thieves - and enriched as I was, I made a tempting target. But I saw only deer, and emerged unchallenged and unharmed if saddle-sore, and so numbed that I could barely feel the reins. Before me were fields as Huginn had said, with a mist rising, hence I could not see far. Yet there was no choice other than to ride on and trust to luck. Whereupon, a few minutes later, I came upon the farmstead.

It was small: a huddle of low buildings, approached by a narrow track; smoke rose from a rooftop. I halted Kappi and peered ahead, squinting in the early light: could this truly be where Lord Feng was living – even hiding? The King's brother, who now ruled Jutland as his steward? Moreover, was this where Gertrude came in secret to keep tryst with him? The ride had been long, though in daylight it might have been made in half the time I'd taken...

I pushed such thoughts away; I was too tired for reasoning. I shook myself and dismounted, mighty stiff in body and limb. I would lead Kappi forward, for what I hoped were our last paces before we both found food and rest. Up the track we walked, I should say trudged. Through a gate in a fence of withies, past a barn with a few chickens scratching nearby, the house facing us across a yard spattered with cow-shit - then a shout that brought me up short.

'Stop! What's your business?'

From the shadow of the barn a sentry appeared: stout as an oak and likely as dense, wearing a poniard and holding a wooden billet. Kappi jerked his rein and stamped, obliging me to soothe him. Meanwhile the guard drew near, holding out his billet in a threatening manner.

'Who are you, and what do you want?'

'I carry a message,' I answered, 'for...' I stopped, thinking I'd best not give names. 'For your master,' I went on, tapping my jerkin. 'My orders are to give it to him and no-one else.'

The fellow looked me over to see if I posed a threat, before deciding that I didn't. Whereupon another guard, wearing a sword and less oafish, appeared in the doorway of the house.

'I've ridden all night... ten leagues at least,' I said to the one who challenged me. 'My horse needs food and rest, as do I...'

But he had turned away and was waiting for the other, who had a more important air about him. Neat-bearded and sharp-eyed, he came uncomfortably close to me: one of those who likes to stare the other fellow out to show he's top of the heap. I repeated my words, and at last received a nod.

'This man will see to your horse,' he said, indicating his subordinate. 'You should follow me.' Whereupon, leaving Kappi to be cared for I followed him to the house, under the lintel and into a gloomy passageway. From somewhere at the rear came kitchen noises and a murmur of voices. I was about to raise the topic of breakfast, when the man-at-arms shoved open a door and pointed.

'Wait in here,' he said, and stamped off. So, in a poor humour now, I entered the room, which was bare apart from a chest and some stools, and sat down.

I cannot recall how long I waited: a half hour, perhaps more. There were sounds about the house and footfalls overhead, but no-one came to offer me even a drink of milk. Several times I dozed, only to wake when I found myself slipping off the stool. I was on the point of stretching out on the floor and giving in to my weariness, when at last the door opened and the man-at-arms reappeared.

'You're with me again.'

I followed him up the stairs, dog-tired and with a grumbling stomach. But as we gained the upper floor, I grew wary: could I be certain who the message was for? Uneasily I waited while my guide knocked on a door, then at a command from beyond, threw it open. Light flooded out: both firelight and candlelight, though the morning was advanced. Whereupon, at some further word, he stood aside for me to enter what was clearly a large room. I did so... and stopped.

From a great, four-posted bed with a tasselled canopy and velvet hangings, propped up by pillows and lying beneath a richly-embroidered coverlet, Lord Feng, in a red-and-gold nightgown, gazed at me with interest.

'Poor Yorick,' he murmured in a tone of mingled concern and mockery, after I'd made my bow; only then did it strike me that I'd never heard his voice at close hand. 'You look as if you've toiled across the Alps... are you hungry?'

I coughed, and admitted that I was.

'Will that serve?' He pointed to a table by the window, covered with a rich cloth and laid as for a hearty meal: platters of meat, fish and eggs, together with silver cups. A substantial breakfast, for just one man. Then I noticed two padded chairs, and understood: this finely-appointed room with its ample fireplace, its furnishings, curtains and mirrors, would indeed serve for a trysting-place.

And in truth, a finer parlour for seduction can scarcely be imagined. I could picture the scene, of an evening: Gertrude leaning forward across the table while her lover plied her with wine and delicacies... their laughter, their languid and sensual talk; the kissing of hands, their loins hot with desire in knowledge of what was to follow. Finally, they rise to their feet – would she undress herself, or let him remove her clothing? Whatever the preparations, it would be only a short time before they were in the enormous bed; perhaps Feng would draw the curtains, to closet them both for a glorious consummation. The vision made Yorick's fancies soar, before he succeeded in bringing himself back to the present.

'I would be most grateful, my lord,' I said. 'If I might take some bread and fish, and slake my thirst...'

'Take what you like,' Feng said, in offhand fashion; he lolled in the bed like some ancient emperor. 'But first, don't you have a message for me?'

Walking stiffly towards the bedside, I drew the packet from my jerkin and handed it to him. He glanced at it, then with a gesture bade me retire to the window where I sat down to eat - and rarely had Yorick dined so well. Eagerly I filled my stomach with river perch and eels, wadded with rye bread; nor did I scruple to take a cup of wine - which was not Rhenish, but Malmsey. And soon I was taken back to that time in the presence chamber, when the ailing King Rorik had invited me to share his cup... on a sudden, I stopped chewing. What would he think, if he could see me now? I asked myself. What in thunder was I doing here?

I swallowed, belched, then looked round, half-expecting a reproof. But Lord Feng was so absorbed with his letter, he seemed to have forgotten me. He leaned into the light of the candle at his bedside, peering at it and frowning. Finally, he looked up.

'There will be a reply,' he said; now that I think on it, his voice had a similar timbre to that of pious Mattheus. 'You must tarry while I pen it... have you had enough to eat?' I stood up, nodded and murmured my thanks, waiting to be told to wait downstairs, then found him regarding me through narrowed eyes.

'You're a curious fellow, Yorick,' he observed at last. 'I never knew a jester so trusted.'

Yorick put on his humble face, and remained silent.

'What is it, do you think, that makes you so valued?' Feng asked, raising his eyebrows. 'Surely not your singing voice, for that's indifferent. If you heard the choirs in Rome... the *castrati*... the sweet, soaring melodies, you'd know it too.'

Though somewhat crestfallen, I kept my composure.

'I'm told you're bewitched, as your mother was,' came the next barb. 'Can that be true?'

'I swear not, my lord,' I said at once. 'I was a stable-boy who became a player, learned tumbling and fooling-'

'I know that,' His Lordship said, cutting me short. 'As I know your father was beloved of King Rorik...' a faint smile appeared. 'I suspect that under my brother's rule, your life has altered somewhat.'

I was dumbfounded; this was unexpected, and I knew not how to receive it. Was he trying to draw me further into conspiracy - as if I hadn't seen enough already? The strangeness of my position amazed me: one word to the King, I thought, and this man could lose his life... until I remembered Gertrude, and what she would do to me. And besides, likely I would not be believed - in which case Feng's cuckolding of his brother might appear slightly less reckless. Yet I was in turmoil, my mind busy – what next, I wondered?

'How would you like to serve me instead?' Feng enquired. And when I merely blinked: 'Sometime in the future, I mean... things change, do they not?'

'They do, my lord,' I agreed, after a moment. 'And in ways unfathomable to me.' Seeing he awaited some firmer answer, I added: 'And I would be honoured to serve you... as it seems, I do already.'

'You serve the Queen, Yorick,' came his swift rejoinder; he was no longer smiling. 'You'd be wise to remember that.'

'I do, my lord,' I answered, somewhat wearily. 'Indeed, upon my life I can never forget it.' To which he eyed me sharply for a moment, then grew abrupt.

'You may go now and await the letter, which you'll give to Lord Huginn. My servants will give you some provision for your journey back...' He paused, then: 'Do you want a fuck before you leave?'

I gaped – whereupon Feng gave a shout of laughter. 'I meant with one of the maids... by the gods, what did you think?'

'Most kind, my lord...' I summoned a manly smile. 'I'd be delighted, save that I'm weary and saddle-sore, and...'

I broke off, seeing the look that appeared. I could guess what he thought: was Yorick, the shameless cock-master, passing up such a chance? In vain I searched for excuses – for in truth, rutting was the last thing I desired just then. I was full of stomach and fuddled of brain, still dazed at this turn in my fortunes, the dangers of which might well outweigh the blessings. Though *confiteo:* at times since, I've rued my timidity. I might have seized the moment to advance myself – a chance the Lord Feng seemed to offer. Unhappily I waited, until his dismissal brought relief.

'Very well… you'd better rest before starting back.'

I did rest, stretched out on the floor of the bare room where I'd sat on my arrival; I even managed to sleep. I slept an hour, two at most, before I was roused by the sharp-eyed attendant and ushered out to the yard. There was Kappi, refreshed and ready and looking askance at me, I thought. As I prepared to mount, Feng's steward – if such he was – gave me a sealed packet. There was no name on it.

'There's bread and a cannikin here,' he said, holding out a bag tied at the neck. 'Make haste, before it snows.'

He nodded towards a cloud that threatened, coming in from the west. Then he stood back and watched as I tied the bag to the saddle, got myself horsed and shook the reins. Without looking back I left the farmstead, only now remembering its name: *Saltfelter.*

I would see it again; but as always, I must forbear from leaping ahead.

SIXTEEN

That winter was colder than any I've known, before or since. Streams froze, sheep perished in snowdrifts and blizzards swept Helsingor - and King Hamlet drew up his plans to attack Norway.

I've said we lived now in a fortress, for so it seemed at times. Men-at-arms were housed in the town and at outlying farms, and drills were held in all weathers: a pox on any soldier who showed weakness, the sergeants would bawl. Messengers came and went, carrying orders to the King's commanders further afield, bidding them make ready for the spring campaign. Hence, with the bustle that attended such preparations few would have noticed Yorick, now gloved, hooded and well-attired for riding, setting forth on another journey to distant *Saltfelter*.

Twice more, that winter, I travelled there. The first time was uneventful – and I did not see Lord Feng. I was told by Huginn, when he brought me another sealed packet, that I could put it into the hands of the steward, whose name I never learned, but who now knew me. So during a brief spell of clear weather, this time in daylight, I took the western highway again, making the distance in half the time I'd taken before. At the farmstead I was recognised, given food and drink in the kitchen and handed a message which was already penned – making the letter I'd brought somewhat useless, I thought. After only a short rest I took horse again, and returned to Helsingor the same day.

The second time was somewhat different.

It was a very cold morning, and both Kappi and I were dispirited at having to make the journey. I let him run when I could, slowing only when ice threatened our progress while I hunched in the saddle, swathed in my heaviest clothing. Finally we reached *Saltfelter* once again and passed through the gate; there was no guard, I supposed because of the cold. I dismounted and led Kappi into the stable, which was empty save for an ageing carthorse. Since there was no-one about I fed my own mount, found a pail and, after cracking ice off the top, gave him water to drink. Then I crossed the yard and entered the house, surprised at being unchallenged. I stopped, heard voices from the kitchen and called out. The result was a flurry of sounds as someone scrambled to their feet, and the heavy-set fellow who served as sentry appeared, looking flustered.

'You! What in blazes are you doing here?'

I patted my jerkin to indicate I carried a message, whereupon a frown appeared. 'They never said,' the man muttered. 'Nor do I have orders.'

'The steward,' I said. 'Where is he?'

'Not here,' came the reply, as footsteps sounded, and a blowsy woman in a soiled apron came to the doorway behind him. He turned to her, mumbled something I failed to catch, then faced me again. 'You'd best give the letter to me,' he said in a gloomy voice. 'I'll pass it on when he's next here.'

'I'll not do that,' I said. 'My orders are to give it to the steward. If he's away, then I'll hand it only to your master... His Lordship,' I added. But to that, came another shake of the head.

'He's not here either. First time you rode in was the last time he stayed... second time, the letter you brought was took away by the steward.'

I began to understand: the trysting-place was no longer in use. 'I thought this was one of His Lordship's residences,' I murmured.

There was a snigger from the woman. 'Residences?' she echoed. 'My arse, what fine words for a lackey. This is a farm – his farm.' She jerked her thumb at the other. 'Not that there's much farming gets done any more - His Lordship pays him too well to keep it ready. I'll wager you know what for... you've been upstairs, haven't you?'

I hesitated, recalling my orders had once been not to talk to people here - but then, it was they who were talking to me. 'I have,' I answered. 'There were more servants here that time.'

'Are you calling me a servant?' The woman retorted. 'I'm his wife.'

'Then, I'm honoured.' I stuck on a smile. 'If at a loss. It seems that the... the one who sent the message was unaware His Lordship wasn't here.'

The two looked at each other. 'Sounds odd to me,' the guard-who-was-really-a-farmer muttered. 'And you being the lady's messenger, I thought you'd a' known what's what.' He raised his brows. 'You know who she is, then? For I'm sure we don't.'

Of course you don't, thought I; even Gertrude would not be so careless. She would have arrived veiled, her fine clothes concealed under a riding cloak. 'Yet, you know who His Lordship is,' I said in an idle tone. 'The one who pays you to keep his place of assignation?'

The farmwife gave a snort. 'Yes, we know him. He trusts us – which is more than you seem to do, if you won't leave your letter. Mayhap you should take it back where it came from.'

'I don't think the lady would like that,' I told her. 'In truth, knowing her as I do I expect she'd be very angry, hence-'

'We understand – of course we do,' the farmer broke in then, with a sour look at his wife. 'See now, you must be frozen stiff. Come in the kitchen and warm yourself... I've a pot of ale by the fire.' He gestured to the doorway. 'Then we'll put our heads together, see if we can find a way to hand the message on...' his face clouded. 'Though I can't see how, since we don't know where His Lordship lives.'

I stared at him. 'You don't know?'

He shook his head. 'We swore not to ask, ever since his steward first came here. Still don't know why he picked us to be host and hostess...' he spread his hands. 'But we're poor folk, glad of the business. And he brings his own servants with him, cooks and all... or he used to.' He turned to his wife. 'Will you find some bread and a bit of bacon for our friend?'

She threw me a glance, then left us. Her husband began to follow, but I stayed him. 'She said you know who he is... His Lordship,' I said. And I would have spoken Feng's name, had not the fellow cut me short.

'I do. It's an odd name... I heard he took it from some ruler, in olden times.' And when I waited, he pronounced it.

'Claudius,' he said. 'He's Lord Claudius - the slyest cunt I've known in all my life.'

Two months later, with Helsingor at a pitch of excitement for the coming birth of the Queen's child, Yorick walked outside in early spring and once again mulled over his future.

It had been a curious time. For one thing, though Gertrude's pregnancy drew towards its full term and she was now confined to her chamber for lying-in, instead of tarrying at home her husband had departed on campaign with his army. Though in truth, few were surprised: bringing infants into the world was women's business, and the King had enemies to vanquish. With others I watched him ride out with banners flying, his armour gleaming in the sunlight, helmet and all; he generally wore his beaver up, so men could see his face. Also there on that morning was Huginn who, as the last of the baggage wagons rolled out of the gates, sauntered over to me and planted his staff of office down as if claiming the spot for posterity.

'I'm less than pleased with you, Yorick,' he murmured.

'Indeed, sir?' Yorick had his innocent face ready. 'How have I offended you?'

'Not I, but the Queen,' was his reply. 'In truth, I've observed a change in her manner ever since you returned from your last journey, having failed to deliver her message... yes, I know,' he added, staunching my protest with a raised hand. 'The distance is great, and you had no instruction to go further than *Saltfelter*... nonetheless, I expected a man of your resources to find some solution.'

'Alas - the cold was such, I fear it may have numbed my brain. And I was loth to leave the letter with the farm folk, not knowing how far to trust them.'

'Could you not have hired some horseman to convey it privately – as far as the castle, where sits the ruler of Jutland?'

'There was no-one near, my lord,' I answered sadly. 'And more, there was a blizzard coming, they said. I thought it best to return at once, and so guard the Queen's confidence.'

Huginn opened his mouth, then closed it; in spite of himself, a wry smile appeared. 'Never stuck for an excuse, Yorick,' he muttered.

Wearing my humble face, I waited.

'For all that, you've not been forgotten,' the chamberlain resumed. 'It may be that there's still a place for you here, if not that of a messenger – hence you'll have no need of a mount. The Queen has instructed me to relieve you of the burden of keeping Kappi. There's another whose need is greater... the horse will pass to him.'

'It was no burden, my lord,' I said, stung to the heart. 'And who, might I ask, is the one so favoured?'

'The priest, Father Mattheus,' came the answer. 'His duties have increased, though not being one who attends chapel, I expect you've failed to notice. Doubtless the Queen will have need of his services even more, in the coming year.'

'Doubtless,' Yorick repeated sourly; just then he would have given a great deal for the chance to shove pious Mattheus into the fish-pond.

'And yet...' raising his voice, Huginn fixed me with a hard stare. 'As I said, you are not forgotten. The Queen's child, if he be a son, will need playfellows in time... I speak not only of boys his own age. She wishes him to have games and frolics – to enjoy his childhood, as she herself rarely did. There should be songs and tumbling, she says, all the better for his exercise and to widen his learning... else when his schooling follows, he might turn out a dry pedant like-'

'A chamberlain?' I put in. 'That would indeed disappoint.'

Huginn narrowed his eyes. 'You follow me, I think.'

'I do, my lord,' I said, clearing all expression from my face. 'You wish me to be jester to a mewling infant, the moment he's unswaddled.'

'Unless that infant's a maid,' Huginn replied, undaunted. 'In which case, there'll likely be no need for you at all.'

I looked away; in the distance, the rattle and creaking of baggage carts grew fainter.

'So, you might wish to pray that it isn't – a girl-child, I mean,' the chamberlain continued. 'Why not attend the chapel, as others do... those most loyal to the Queen? I'll leave the notion with you.'

Whereupon, never one to go without a parting remark, he lifted his staff, half-turned and said: 'Since it's no longer wintertime, I'm sure your brain is no longer numbed – nor addled, I hope.' Upon which, he left me.

Now, wandering in the King's garden, I recalled his words in grim solitude. *Confiteo*: I did not enter the chapel, having resolved that I never would. Handsome Mattheus, admired and favoured by everyone, was becoming a stain on my life, I thought, though I had never spoken with him. And in truth, ever since I had returned from *Saltfelter* on that bitter winter's day and given the letter back to Huginn, I'd felt a growing distance between myself and Queen Gertrude. I didn't see her again before she entered confinement, apart from one glimpse of her walking with a maidservant who was not Runa.

So, despite the cheering signs of bud and blossom after the hard winter, I was uneasy that day. In this time of change, when the House of Rorik was giving way to the House of Gerwendil, my future seemed shrouded in fog; I'm no hex, and I saw no star to set a course by. The King would likely triumph over his enemies, I knew – he was a worthy soldier, whose men would follow him through blood and fire. He would return triumphant to greet his new-born child, the beginning of his dynasty. Whereas Yorick, to whom he never gave a thought, seemed to be in the hands of fate once again, his future dependent on whether the fruit of the royal loins were male or female; as for the notion that it may be the fruit of another set of loins altogether, I did not dare to dwell on it. After spending an hour or more in idle rumination, I went to the kitchens where I was able to distract the maids long enough to seize a flagon of wine and make off with it. And that night, I got seriously drunk.

It had been a while since I'd indulged to excess. Alone in my chamber, I downed the contents of the flagon until I was sodden: full-blown, falling-down drunk, the room fizzing about me. I grew reckless, of course: hang the *mareridt* if it came again, I swore; my life was so wretched, I was beyond caring. I recall tugging Makan's old shawm out of its bag and trying to coax a tune from it, before falling on my rump spluttering with laughter. I threw the window wide, I remember, and bellowed some choice crudities at the moon, then reeled away, tripping over my own feet. For a while I lost the flagon, before finding it on its side, almost empty. Seated on my pallet I drained the last drops, then gazed blearily at my sputtering rush light, which was about to go out.

I found myself frowning: dizzy as I was, the moment seemed charged with something unseen but potent. I thought of Makan, as I so often did, but could not hear his voice. I thought of Gitte, but she was only a memory now. And yet I grew fearful, so that after a while I struggled to my feet, swaying where I stood. Something was in the room, I believed... or was it merely a fancy brought on by the drink? I peered about, but saw no-one - and then my gorge rose. I lurched towards the window, intending to lean out - but I never reached it, thanks to a whoreson beam which chose that moment to crack me on the forehead. The blow shook me from skull to toe-bone, lights flew about my head as I fell to the floor... and most curiously, a sweet voice seemed to be singing, some old air I knew but couldn't name. The voice was familiar – and as I sank into oblivion, I believed I knew it: Runa's voice, lifted in song, as she'd once taught me troubadours' melodies behind the brewing-house wall; it seemed a very long time ago.

And Yorick should have known what had befallen her, but he was a drunken fool who slept like a dead man until morning, when he awoke on the floor with a parched mouth and a throbbing head, dimly aware of noises... which slowly resolved themselves to the ringing of bells and the sound of cheering coming through the open casement. Shakily, fighting nausea, he clambered to his feet and staggered to the window, but could see little. Whereupon he got himself to the door, out to the passage and lurched down the stairs to accost the first person he saw: Thura the Beanpole, seemingly in a great hurry. But what brought him up short was the sight of her customary sour face, wreathed in a smile.

'It's over, Yorick,' she said. 'The Queen's given birth, sooner than expected - but all is well!'

I peered at her, before the news restored my wits in a trice.

'Is it a boy?' I blurted, but she was already hurrying off. In a froth of anticipation, I made my way to the kitchen where there was a gathering of servants, talking excitedly. As I blundered in, heads turned towards me.

'The Queen's child, is it male?' I demanded - and on receiving an answer, sagged in relief.

'It is,' someone said. 'By the grace of God she is blessed with a fine, well-formed boy. Our new prince – the Prince of Denmark.'

Murmurs of approval followed. No-one seemed inclined to do any work - least of all Yorick, who got himself to the table where in earlier times he'd sat with Makan. There I slumped, dizzy with the realisation that I was to be the playfellow of this Prince; another turning, I thought vaguely. My mouth being dry as tinder, I was looking round for ale or even water to sate my thirst, when someone appeared at the door to the kitchen garden: one of the grooms, the same who'd once called me to the stable to take the reins of Kappi... and at his expression, I frowned.

'It's Runa,' the fellow muttered. 'We found her at the foot of the west turret.'

My heart smacked against my ribs.

'Neck's broke,' he went on. 'Looks like she fell from a casement. Dead as you like - what a turnabout, eh? One is born, another dies the same night.'

I sagged as the realisation swept over me. I had heard her - heard her singing to me in the night, drunk as I was... tears welled, stinging my eyes, but I hid them. Nobody paid me any heed: the sight of Yorick with head in hands, paying the price for a night's drinking, was common enough. Hence I barely heard the gasps of dismay as the groom delivered his tidings to the servants; barely heard the cries which broke out among the maids.

What I did hear, when I at last stumbled outdoors, was scant mention of Runa. Instead there was excited chatter about the Queen's good fortune; how she was already sitting up and speaking, seemingly in excellent spirits; how couriers were leaving to carry the news across the realm - and to the King, wherever he was. How the Lord Huginn and others had gathered at Gertrude's bedside to witness the child's sex and good health, and were now conferring in the presence chamber.

And for the first time I heard the Prince's name: in honour of his father, it was to be Hamlet.

SEVENTEEN

So began Yorick's years of service to the young Prince of Denmark: Lord Hamlet, whose growth from suckling babe to sweet-natured boy would henceforth bind his loyal fool to Helsingor, to the extent that he no longer desired to leave it. Would that he had, I might say now: for in truth I'd have been spared a turbulent journey that has brought me at last to this pitiful case: sick, helpless and all but forgotten by everyone from the King and Queen down to the lowliest lackey. I'm no better than a prisoner – have I not said so? That my chamber is guarded like a cell, while powers elsewhere take their time in deciding what to do with me? *Confiteo* - two things, and two only, keep my spirits from sinking beyond hope of recovery: the writing of my Tale, which others may one day read and understand; and the hope that Prince Hamlet thinks of me and may yet come - bringing if not salvation, then at least his golden presence, his voice and his boyish laughter, to comfort me in what days I have left.

Well, a pox on everyone; I'll go on, and speak of my dearest Runa.

There was no burial at Helsingor, no grim spadework for Absalom the son of Agnaar to do. Runa's slim body, shrouded and wrapped, was sent to the village where she had grown up, to be interred by her aged mother; hence Yorick had no chance to stand by the grave and speak some last words. But then, what words could I have uttered save those of regret - for the good and loving wife I might have had, if only King Rorik had lived a while longer? Indeed, it seemed that in those months that followed, months that stretched into years, regret was all I knew: a bitter ruing of what could and should have been.

For a long time I mourned her, dwelling on memories, however brief, of the moments we had together. I knew now that the well of good fortune spoken of by the hex Edela had indeed run dry; once a clown and a Favoured Fool, I was become a poor excuse for both. All that buoyed me was the knowledge that, as Prince Hamlet emerged from infancy and took his first steps – which he was quick to do, being a lively and spirited child – I was to be the boy's jester and his playfellow, which could well be the saving of Yorick.

And see now, Hamlet was beloved - make no mistake in that. From first sight of him as a babe that summer, when he was brought out of his nursery to be admired by all, he was the kingdom's joy. Even the dour face of the King, once he was returned triumphant from his Norway campaign, softened with pride and pleasure when he beheld his son. Moreover, it was soon known that the very day of Hamlet's birth was the same one on which the King had defeated Fortinbras: a good omen indeed.

And in truth there was a lightening of the mood thereafter at Helsingor – across all of Denmark, now that we were at peace and the army dispersed. As the year went by it became less of a fortress and more a seat of government, with new laws made and new councillors engaged under the shrewd eye of Lord Huginn. After another year Helsingor had grown as the King had promised, with envoys from other lands coming to visit… and all the while, Yorick waited in a kind of limbo.

And yet, I was seldom downcast. There was time for frolicking – especially with Bodil of the brewing-house. Bodil, flaxen of hair and ruddy of cheek, came to my chamber now and then, until her whoreson father the brew-master put a stop to it, declaring Yorick unfit as a suitor. To which Yorick might have answered, when did I ever speak of marriage? More, there were opportunities for fooling, if not at Court: King Hamlet, seemingly at Gertrude's behest, had little time for me. I would amuse the stablemen with my stock of bawdy jests, or the kitchen folk in exchange for a mug or two…

But *confiteo*: I am failing to *recall the impurity of my life's past*. In truth it was a time of idleness, as I waited to be called to better service. Yet when that day came – a day of autumn, when Hamlet was perhaps three and a half years old - it was not as I'd expected.

It was not Queen Gertrude who summoned me – not that I ever thought she would – nor even Huginn, but a new face: a gangling, weasel-faced scholar who announced himself as the

Prince's tutor. He had once been a tutor to the young Queen, he informed me, and had now been engaged by Gertrude with the approval of her chamberlain. He would be taking up his duties in a few months, in a new schoolroom which was being fitted out especially. His name was Rathulf, he said, explaining that it was derived from the Latin word *ratus*, meaning 'fixed' or 'reliable', or even 'sure' - which was his first mistake as far as Yorick was concerned. For as I was quick to inform him, Rathulf was in fact an old Danish name meaning nothing much at all.

'To the untrained mind, perhaps,' the tutor murmured, blinking at me. 'If you understood the tongues of the ancients you would know otherwise – but no matter. *Videlicet*, that is to say, etymology is not among the topics the King and Queen expect you to promote, Master Yorick. I'm given to understand you will be the Prince's companion in matters of, shall we say, a sportive nature: running and leaping, and so forth. Have I been misinformed?'

Wearing no particular face, Yorick informed him that he had not.

'Well then, can we agree on the division of our labours? The Prince is in his fourth year of life, and in my opinion there's no time to waste in laying the foundations of his education – the King and Queen are in agreement on that. I am drawing up a table of learning – letters and figures, followed by logic and rhetoric and so forth - though I realise this be of small interest to you. I will have him for the mornings after he's come from chapel - the Queen is insistent he attends service each day. Then after he's taken nuncheon, you may serve him in the afternoons – unless I have cause to keep him longer. Thoroughness is my watchword, Yorick... that, and diligence.'

By the gods, thought I, *the boy's doomed.* 'Do you not think a growing lad needs exercise, Master Rathulf?' I enquired. 'The King will want him to learn skills befitting a soldier and a leader, and such won't be learned in a schoolroom. He'll engage men to train him in martial matters, like how to handle sword and poniard...'

But at the look that appeared, I trailed off. His manner, it struck me, was of a man far older than his years, which could not have been more than ten above mine. Having fixed me with what I would come to know as his reproving face, he attempted a smile.

'A Prince must first acquire wisdom and judgement,' Rathulf droned. 'What profit is there in commanding an army, without the knowledge of how best to employ it? I might direct you to the works of men like Tacitus and Sallust, wherein are found the exploits of Caesar and other great generals of the past... but that would be fruitless, would it not? For a fellow like you, I mean.'

By now I was taut in every limb. Here was another, I thought, who might benefit from a shove into the pond, ideally when there was a crust of ice upon it. But I was caught, as always: a prisoner of ignorance and servitude. Being forced to endure tiresome Rathulf in the years ahead would be a sore trial, unless I found ways to deal with him. A strong drink was called for, to ponder the matter.

'True enough, master,' I said, summoning my cheerful face. 'Yet perhaps I could remind you of the words of other men, like the great fool Makan, beloved of our late King Rorik. He would have told you of the value of laughter and merriment as a balm to many ills – the sheer pleasure, say, of watching some dry pedant slip and fall on his arse. But I'll await instruction as to when I might take the Prince out for some sport, taking care he doesn't get any wisdom or judgement from it. Now with your leave, I'm in sore need of a good shit.'

So ended my first meeting with Rathulf, who would in time acquire other names. *Corambis* was one of them - dubbed by none other than Prince Hamlet himself. That too is a Latin word, the Prince said, meaning 'twice present', or something like it. Twice present as in 'two-faced' – since in the years to come, neither Hamlet nor I could ever be certain which one of them would turn up. At risk of *digression* (mark that!), let me say this: there are men who are good-natured and kindly in private, but adopt a stiff and dour manner in public discourse, the better to achieve their ends. While others are stiff and dour by nature, yet think it better to get their way through gentle persuasion. Rathulf was of the latter kind - even if both sides would meld later into one glum-faced, prating creature, a master of fluff and flattery. But as he would say, *satis, et legere*.

Winter passed, giving way to a spring of high winds, and there were changes at Helsingor. For one, the Queen was seen to ride out once again, leaving the Prince in the care of his nurses. Sometimes she went with the King to admire new buildings which were rising - particularly a church they had bespoken, which was to be blessed by the Bishop. Yet at other times she rode alone, which aroused my curiosity. Would she dare to visit Lord Feng now, I wondered? Such indiscretion would have been most reckless – but knowing Gertrude, and having seen their trysting-place with my own eyes, I believed it possible.

And yet, what use was there in speculation? I was still her creature – indeed, the more I'd learned since the first time she wielded her power over me, I began to think, the more dangerous was my position. I had no protector – certainly not Hamlet the elder, who never called on me even though I was yet, in name at least, the King's jester. Nor Huginn, who never called me either, though at times I would see him observing me from a distance. And surely not Rathulf, who regarded me as a dolt and a hindrance to his mission of implanting great learning in the mind of the young Prince. Hence my only course was to keep out of sight until lessons began in earnest, after Hamlet's fourth birthday.

And it was about that time that Helsingor received a most unexpected visitor: Lord Feng, who since his pilgrimage to Rome had taken the name Claudius, arrived to pay homage to the King and Queen, and to view his celebrated nephew.

I learned of it late one afternoon, when I was in the kitchen garden entertaining two young maids who were recently come to Helsingor, and who found my stock of jests both fresh and amusing. One, somewhat heavy and plain, was named Gunhild; the other, well-formed and decidedly alluring, was Yiva. Hence it was Yiva to whom I directed my best efforts, thinking to entice her to my chamber that night with a jug of something. They were country girls from down south, still overawed by the royal splendour of their new home. To their eyes even Yorick must have appeared somewhat grand, neither of them having met a King's jester before – a notion he was not slow to exploit.

'It's true I have my own quarters,' I said airily. 'Such privacy is rare, let alone such comfort. Then, good King Rorik was a wise and generous monarch, who granted me many a favour. When I sang for him, I could bring a tear to his eye... what nights of revelry I've seen, in the High Hall. The tales I could tell you – some of them a trifle bawdy for your ears perhaps, but then again...'

'I'd like to hear them,' Gunhild said, with a sly look.

'What of you?' I said to Yiva. 'I've a notion you might prefer a song – a sweet lay of romance, such as the Frankish troubadours make. I have a goodly store of such, in here.' I tapped my head and directed a smile at her.

'So I've heard,' Yiva said, after a moment. 'I also heard you were taught them by a maidservant who jumped out of a window.'

I flinched; ever the one to malign me, this had to be Thura's work.

'That's sad,' Gunhild said, her mouth hanging open. 'Did she pine for her lover? Was he a soldier slain in the wars?'

'She pined,' I said, 'because she was forbidden to marry...'

But I broke off, sick at heart. For years I'd tried not to dwell on the knowledge that Runa's death - which everyone knew was by her own hand, though it was rarely spoken of – had come about because she was unable to escape Gertrude's tyranny. And in a way the fault was mine – it was useless to blame Rorik's untimely demise. Was this, I wonder now, why I so often dulled my senses with drink? I turned away, producing a response from the maids that could not have been more different.

'You're a sorry fellow, Master Yorick,' Yiva said. 'I know naught of your dealings with the one who taught you her songs, but I don't like what I hear... nor do I like you much.' Following which, she turned and went back inside the kitchen.

'Don't pay her any mind,' Gunhild said. 'I never do.'

And when I faced her, with a tangle of feelings unsought and unwanted, she touched my sleeve and assumed a leery smile. 'I said I'd like to hear your tales, up in that chamber of yours. Tomorrow night, say, when my work's done here? Then if you make me laugh, we'll have a fuck – does that suit?'

Her hand slid downwards, to my thigh... and *confiteo*, it was breeches-tightening enough. And when all's said and sifted, who was Yorick to turn up his nose at that? A friendless wretch, and a whoreson mad rogue, as some called him – who as a youth, once had the gall to believe that the Princess herself, now Queen of Denmark, had true affection for him? And more – that he was even the bastard son of King Rorik? Pock-faced as she was, Gunhild was the only maid who'd favoured me in months... with a sigh, I took her hand.

'It suits,' I answered. 'And if you can lay your hands on a jug of Rhenish, tuck it under your apron and bring it along, it would suit even more.'

She returned to her work, throwing a smile over her shoulder as she went. Yorick lingered, trying to force aside his melancholy and think of the morrow, when he'd explore the ample body of brazen Gunhild. On a whim, I thought to walk to the stables and visit Kappi, which had become my habit of late. Yet I did not, for a trumpet sounded, followed by the noise of a commotion from the courtyard. With others I made my way there, in time to see a small group of horsemen enter the gates. And at their head, splendidly attired, was Lord Feng – whereupon scarcely knowing why, I stepped back into shadow, not wishing to be seen.

But I watched. I saw servants hurry out to hold the horses, as His Lordship – I'll call him Claudius now, as he's been known since – as Claudius dismounted with his followers. And I was reminded of another day, long ago, when I'd stood with Makan to watch his arrival for the betrothal feast, and believed I saw the future husband of Gertrude; how wrong could I be? Once again, I observed him from a distance; I saw his smile, his courteous greeting of Huginn who had emerged from a doorway with his staff of office. I saw a packhorse laden with what would be gifts for the King and Queen, and likely for Prince Hamlet too. I watched until the party made their way indoors before sloping off to my chamber, where I slumped down on my pallet.

What was that feeling I had, of grim portent? To this day I'm uncertain of its cause; I believe it had little to do with the hard words Yiva had spoken, and more to do with a memory of the last time I'd seen Claudius, lying in the splendour of his great bed at *Saltfelter*, asking me if it was true that I was bewitched. This visit of his, I thought, was more than one of mere courtesy to King Hamlet: if it was congratulations he brought for the birth of a son, then why had he not come sooner? More, knowing what I did about the cuckolding his brother, how did he and Gertrude mean to conduct themselves under the King's gaze? Had she known of this visit – had she even willed it?

It was beyond the reasoning of Yorick, he decided, when he rose at last with his stomach calling for sustenance; all he wished for was to sleep soundly that night, untroubled by the *mareridt*, in readiness for what would follow.

But he did not; nor did he have the chance to explore Gunhild's body the following night either. For while he was taking supper in the kitchens, an order came from Lord Huginn that he least expected: that the King's jester should attend him, his Queen, the Prince Hamlet and guests in the High Hall the next evening, to provide entertainment at their feast. The Lord Claudius, it seemed, had made the request himself, to which His Highness, out of kinship and the devotion he bore towards his brother, had agreed.

And Yorick spent the night in turmoil, without even a pot of ale for company.

EIGHTEEN

The night of the feast was momentous, memorable - and melodious. Behold my use of words: have I not come far, from my time as a grubby stable-lad? It's called *alliteration*, just one of the things I learned once I began to be taught... but I'll come to that anon. Let me tell of the supper that the King held in honour of the brother to whom he was now, it seemed, reconciled; and in honour of his son Prince Hamlet, who though yet a child would sit at the High Table beside his father. It was to be a celebration, if one arranged in haste following the sudden arrival of Lord Claudius. There had been no time to hire musicians, hence Yorick was to sing and divert the company, though without falling to his well-known crudities; that was made clear by Huginn when he accosted me that evening.

'Think of this as a chance to redeem yourself,' the chamberlain said. 'And smarten yourself up, too – you look like a beggar.'

'Some might say I'm little more than that, My Lord,' I answered.

'Indeed. Some might also say you're fortunate to be here at all, with bed and board at the King's expense. It's time you earned your keep. What do you propose to offer him tonight?'

'Songs... perhaps a rhyme or two. Whatever suits the company.'

'Nothing too bawdy – I've no need to point that, have I?'

Yorick let him understand that he had not, while conjuring up an image of a different sort of point, with which to puncture Huginn's fat gut.

'Good...' he peered at me. 'I hear you're to sport with the Prince soon, provide some boyish rough-and-tumble and the like. As you may know, it's at the Queen's behest. Betwixt ourselves, I heard the King was against it.'

By the gods, thought I – *does she still twist him like a straw?* 'Yet His Highness is a soldier,' I said. 'He must understand the need for relief from book-learning.' *And the need for relief from his tutor*, I could have added.

'He does,' the chamberlain retorted. 'And be under no illusion about your role. Better men than you will instruct the Prince in horsemanship, fencing and the like. Be assured also that your actions will be observed. The King likes to hear young Hamlet's account of what he's done each day, and in detail.'

I donned my compliant face - whereupon words sprang up and flew out of my mouth before I could stop them. 'Was it at the King's invitation that Lord Claudius is come to Helsingor?' I asked. 'Or the Queen's?'

A look of annoyance crossed Huginn's features. 'Beggars ought not to ask questions, Yorick,' he said. 'Where I come from, they're beaten for less. You'd do yourself good service to remember that.'

'I do, sir,' I answered at once. 'And my loyalty to Her Highness is undimmed as always... I've no need to assure you of that, have I?'

A silence fell. And though I rued my rashness, the truth stood between us, unvarnished and unspoken: this man was privy to Gertrude's secret as I was – the one who'd first handed me a purse along with her letter to her lover that windy autumn night, and sent me off to *Saltfelter*. We exchanged looks, before Huginn leaned close on a sudden, making me flinch.

'Have a care, Yorick,' he muttered. 'Or your fate may be worse than even your wildest fancies could conjure. Now, I'll not keep you longer - are you content?'

Well now, I was far from content. But since I was about to go to work once again, I meant to make a passable fist of it.

The High Hall was abuzz, or so I might have said back in King Rorik's time. In truth it was not – abuzz, that is. There was no glittering crowd packing the hall, sending the noise of their laughter to the roof-beams. Instead there was a subdued company, at the High Table only. Yorick tasted the mood the moment he entered, bounding forward to doff his hat and make his bow, smile firmly in place. There was the King, stately and well-attired, though looking somewhat less taut than usual. Likely the reason was the sweet, handsome boy who sat beside him: Prince Hamlet in a fine broidered tunic, his golden hair tidily fashioned. My heart warmed at sight of him... could it be because he bore small resemblance to his mother? He had none of her features, but bore the looks of Gerwendil's line; I forbear to guess which of that ruler's sons he took after. It was enough for me - it is still – that he was of a happy disposition: alert and ready for discourse with anyone. My hopes rose for the times we would have together - but for now, my duty lay elsewhere.

Aside from the Queen, who was seated on the other side of Hamlet, and Claudius, who sat on the other side of his brother (was this by the King's order, I wondered?), Huginn was there, with Rathulf in a dowdy scholar's gown beside him. Already, I suspected, the tutor's discourse had bored the wily chamberlain, who was giving full attention to his platter. And apart from a few lords who had come at short bidding, there was another: Mattheus in his priest's robes, pink-faced and beardless, eying me with frank curiosity. It was the first time he and I had locked eyes, though I cannot claim any meaning passed between us. Besides, there was no time to think: once again, after so long an absence, I was on.

'What will you have, Highness?' I asked of the King. 'A song of heroes as you once would, or one of romance?' I smiled briefly at the Queen, but discerned little from her expression: it struck me as one of boredom, or even displeasure. I refrained from looking at Claudius: I'd no wish to know what humour he was in. I was wary of him now, even more than I was of Gertrude.

'I thought to let you choose, *Hofnar*,' King Hamlet said, more cordially than he'd ever addressed me before. 'You had a goodly song once, of the youth who met the *huldra*, did you not?' He turned to his brother. 'Would that please you, My Lord?'

With eyes lowered, I waited. Why was it, I wondered, that I feared to meet Claudius's gaze? To my dismay the silence grew: was he waiting for me to look at him? I believed I felt his will, bent against mine; or perhaps it was mere fancy. At last, when a chill had fallen across the company, there came an answer.

'If it pleases you, sir, then that's enough,' Claudius said with a smile. 'But what says our royal sister? Should not the first song be the Queen's choice?' With a purposeful movement he leaned forward, looking beyond both his brother and the Prince to where Gertrude sat – and now Yorick saw it.

She was neither bored nor merely displeased: she was seething with anger, and reining it in with difficulty.

'What need have you to ask, My Lord?' Gertrude said. 'The King has made his wish known, and who am I to gainsay it?'

A moment followed, as taut as any Yorick had known, whereupon it dawned on him that he was to be the saviour of the occasion. With another bow, I breathed in deeply and began the song of the *huldra* which, though it had not passed my lips in years, was fresh enough: I'd made sure of recalling it in my chamber. And it went well, even if some of my audience paid no heed but continued to stuff their mouths, Huginn and Rathulf among them. But a pox on them: the royal party were satisfied, it seemed – and none more so than the little Prince.

'A goodly tale!' Hamlet cried, clapping his hands. 'I like the fool well, father – will he sing again?'

'He would be delighted, Highness,' I said quickly. 'What will you have?'

When reply came, however, it was not from the Prince, but from Claudius.

'What about a bawdy rhyme, to tickle my young nephew?' He said, looking not at his brother but at me. 'I recall the one about a cow that farts perfume, which once set the table on a roar – do you know it still, *Hofnar*?'

I swallowed, my mouth dry; what wouldn't I have given for a slurp of wine from one of their silver goblets? Swiftly I glanced from King to Queen, to Claudius and back to the King – only for the matter to be decided by none of them.

'Why, yes!' Cried the Prince. 'I would hear that – can I, father?'

All eyes turned to the older Hamlet, who hesitated before giving a nod. 'Why should you not?' Turning to his brother, he said: 'My son will hear far worse when he moves among men of war... I'll not have him shy from the coarse nature of the world, as some do.'

With that he signalled to Yorick, who mastered himself and delivered the ballad of the fragrant cow. Seldom had he been so glad to get to the end of a piece – and seldom had he had such a response: grudging applause from some, looks of disapproval from the likes of Huginn and Rathulf, a broad smile from Claudius - and squeals of laughter from the young Prince. He stood on his chair, clapping and smiling at me.

And what relief was that to the breathless Yorick – for I knew then that Hamlet and I would be merry companions; knew that I could make him laugh as Makan had made me laugh, sport with him as Makan had with me, carry him on my back as he had carried me. The notion of turning such friendship to profit - I swear it – never arose: only the knowledge that I would make a playfellow of this charming boy, and make myself whole again. What pranks, I thought, what buffoonery would we devise – what mischief!

Aglow with pleasure and fresh hopes, I made my bow to the Prince; I had no eyes for anyone else. What matter if I'd brought royal opprobrium on my head, let alone that of tedious Rathulf or grim-faced Huginn? I'll not speak of Mattheus, whose face bore no expression - but I'll speak of Gertrude.

Gertrude, while her young son remained on his chair grinning at Yorick, rose grandly from her seat, waited for a servant to pull it away, then walked from the table without a word. And Yorick remembered, as would the King and his brother, how she'd done the same on the night her betrothal was announced, years before; the difference this time was that nobody watched her leave, nor did anyone follow. Instead they kept their eyes lowered, each waiting for another to speak... and who else should it be, but Claudius?

'Nobly done, *Hofnar*,' he said with a faint smile. 'Take this for your reward.'

He dug in his gown, found a coin and tossed it in my direction. I caught it and bowed, breathing out in relief. Whatever might follow, just then I hadn't a care; it was the most important performance I gave, and it remains so still.

And less than a week afterwards, I spent my first afternoon with Hamlet.

It was a day of heavy rain, so that my hopes of taking him outdoors were quashed. But no matter: as soon as I attended the Prince I saw he was eager for sport, no doubt restless after his morning lesson with Rathulf. We went to the High Hall, where I swung him up on my shoulders and carried him back and forth – whereupon, to my surprise, he made a farting noise with his mouth and giggled.

'It's lucky I didn't fart with my fundament, Yorick,' he said. 'For it would be no sweet perfume like the cow in your tale - you would be most sorry for it!'

'Indeed I would, Highness,' I answered from below. 'I'd choke with the fumes.'

Hamlet chuckled again. 'I did one this morning,' he said.

'What, a fart?'

'Yes, and Rathulf chided me. He said 'twas not a princely thing to do.'

'Did he?' I felt a smile coming on. 'Well now, mayhap prancing about like this is none too princely either. Shall I set you down?'

'No! Bear me outside, to the stables – I would see the horses.'

'Alas, the rain is too fierce, Highness. You'll get soaking wet, and I'll be in trouble with your nurse for causing it.'

'Then where can we go?'

I decided on the kitchen: it could do no harm, and his presence would cheer the maids. I might even get a drink off them – and there was Gunhild, yet to be boarded after our tryst was delayed. So I set off through the corridors with Hamlet on my back, a willing horse and his rider, to the amusement of the sentries. On entering the kitchen with its aroma of roasting pork, I halted, made a trumpet sound and announced the arrival of Prince Hamlet, on his new charger Yorick.

The result was gladdening: exclamations of delight followed by curtseys, and a surge of female bodies in our direction. Hamlet was pleased by his reception, accepting praise for his horsemanship with good grace. Drinks and sweetmeats appeared – which Yorick was not slow to share.

'What's this?' I demanded, after tasting a cup of watered wine. 'A prince's mount merits only the best – have you no Malmsey?'

'A prince's mount gets water, along with oats and hay like any other nag,' someone said. 'Shall we send to the stables?'

It was Thura, hands on hips, regarding me with a stony look. She may have ruled the kitchen maids by then, but today she was powerless: from Favoured Fool, Yorick was on the way to being Prince's Companion, and he was eager to show it.

'Do you hear that, Highness?' I asked in a shocked voice. 'They would feed your horse with mere hay and water – an outrage.'

But Hamlet was eager to be moving again. 'Has the rain not ceased?' He asked. 'We could go to the stables yet...' he looked round as one of the maids appeared beside us: Gunhild.

'I believe it has ceased, Highness,' she said with a smile. Bending close to me, she muttered: 'I'll come to you tonight – be ready.' Then she bobbed her curtsey and backed away – colliding with Thura who stood stiff as her namesake: a true beanpole.

'Have you no work to do?' She snapped. As Gunhild retreated smartly, she levelled her gaze at me. 'Puffed up once again, Yorick,' she said. 'Be careful where you tread - even a royal mount may stumble.'

Whereupon with a curtsey to the Prince, she stood back and waited for us to leave. Which we did, galloping out to the kitchen garden – but not before I had blown a lip-fart in her direction, much to the amusement of Hamlet.

That was the first of many good days we spent together, through spring and summer, gambolling about the palace and its surrounds. We would go to the stables and feed the horses, and someone would set the Prince astride a pony while I shared a mug with the men. We would go to the fish-pond and dangle a baited line, sometimes hooking a carp which Hamlet liked to take to the kitchens, demanding it be served up for his supper. In the King's garden we played hide-and-seek, which always ended when Yorick was discovered crouching behind a tree. Sometimes other children, sons and daughters of Helsingor's grooms and artisans, were allowed to join the Prince for games, though there was always a guard nearby to watch over him. And in truth, word must have spread that I was somewhat lax with the boy, even careless, as when he came indoors grimed and tousled, his clothes in disarray. Not that it troubled Hamlet, who was always pleased to greet me and, it seemed, to put aside what he had learned in his morning's lesson. *Confiteo:* I see now that this was part of my undoing, though back then I was too contented and too reckless to see it. I should have taken heed that evening, towards the end of our first summer's frolicking, when Rathulf called me to the schoolroom. There, seated at his table with its heap of dusty books, he proceeded to deliver his lecture.

'Your task is to exercise the Prince in manly fashion, as to leap-frog and ball-games and so forth,' he began, fixing me with his reproving look. 'Instead, it's been observed that you allow him to indulge in rough sports and fooleries, not to mention banter with stablemen and the like. Your pranks are too broad - I even hear that you walked on your hands before him and made lewd sounds with your nether parts. It's unseemly – and I'm displeased.'

'What of the King and Queen?' I enquired. 'Are they displeased?'

'Would you be good enough to stick to the point?' Rathulf retorted. 'I am his tutor, charged with delivering such learning as befits a prince – likely a future king. Such folk as you dally with are his servants and subjects, not his friends.' He paused to let the idiot Yorick absorb his wisdom, then:

'It's been suggested that some more fitting companions – boys of noble birth – be brought in to be his playfellows. Such as may one day accompany him to a university, wherever that may be. A boy of fine wit needs to spend time with others of similar mind, rather than…'

He trailed off, allowing me to supply the missing words: *a clod like you*, perhaps? But Yorick wasn't about to give him satisfaction.

'He seems glad enough to sport with me, and with those we encounter,' I said. 'To my mind he's somewhat young to be spending all morning at lessons – he's eager to cavort, and to clear the cobwebs from his mind.'

'Your pardon?' Rathulf blinked at me. 'Are you attempting to tell me what's best for my pupil?'

'By the gods, would I dare?' I replied. 'I'm a mere jester, and that's what I do – jest.'

A pained expression appeared. 'And do you believe that jesting and fooling are more important to the Prince than his learning to read and to write?'

'Stab me if the thought ever passed through my head,' I answered, with a horrified look. 'May the forces of dullness and duty prevail, for ever.'

Rathulf sighed, and changed tack. 'I was of the opinion you and I were agreed on our apportionment of labour,' he said. 'And your entertaining of the boy does you some credit – I've not said otherwise. Can you not curb your more robust tendencies, and think over what I *have* said?'

I managed a nod – upon which he delivered tidings that made me blink.

'You may think me a dull sort, Yorick,' he intoned. 'I was brought up to regard duty as a man's chief aim in life… duty and obedience. Yet in former times, I was not always so inclined. I suffered much extremity for love… though by God's grace I'm now blessed with the finest wife a man may hope for. All of my joy stems from her.'

'You have a wife?' I blurted.

'A wife, who's by God's grace will soon compound my joy by presenting me with a child,' Rathulf replied, with an attempt at a smile. 'If it's a son, I will choose his name from the classics. Perhaps one day he too can be a companion to the Prince; one lives in hope.'

Whereupon he coughed and recovered himself, and we soon parted.

I spoke of it that night to Gunhild, both of us unclothed on my pallet, as we had often been that summer.

NINETEEN

'I've heard about Rathulf,' Gunhild said. 'They say his wife's rarely seen and never speaks. Likely he does enough blabbing for the two of them.'

Being dry of mouth and sweaty, for the night was warm, I reached for my cup, took a drink and passed it to her.

'I've been hearing other things too,' she went on, wiping her lips with a hand. 'Like how your first fuck was a kitchen-wench like me – Ragnhild, was it?'

'I never dwell on what's past,' I said. 'I don't ask about your first – was he poor-sighted, or just drunk?' I yelped as she grabbed my chest-hair and pulled it.

'Mind your mouth. He wasn't such a drunkard as you, I'll say that for him.' She thought for a while, then: 'You're your own worst enemy, Yorick. You've a loose tongue - you offend folk. You need to watch your neck.'

I turned to face her. 'Is this something else you've heard?'

'They say the Queen despises you.'

'She despises everyone. You should have seen her when she was younger.'

'Is it true she once got you alone in a room, with not even a servant present?'

'There was a servant present – me,' I said at once. 'And do you think I was such a dolt as to do anything improper? I'd have been hanged within the hour.'

'I saw a man hanged once,' Gunhild said. 'His cock stood up like a pole when he dropped.'

'I've heard of such,' I said, keen to alter the topic. 'And talking of which…'

But she was distracted that night; when I reached for her breast, she shoved my hand away. 'That's all you do talk of, most of the time,' she sighed. 'You who bide with the Prince. You could be more than you are… don't you wish for it?'

'More?' I blew a lip-fart; it had become a habit, since it generally made Prince Hamlet chuckle. 'I'm even lower born than you, and count myself lucky. I nearly died at my birth –

169

they called for a priest, but none would come. If I'd not lived through that night, my grave would have been a pit in the woods...' I paused. 'It could be yet.'

'I thought you never dwelled on what's past,' Gunhild said.

We were silent for a while, then she turned to look me in the eye. 'What was it passed betwixt you and Lord Claudius, then?'

I frowned. It was months since Claudius' visit, and the night of the banquet when he'd embarrassed the King and angered the Queen. I had no notion what came of it, since he'd left Helsingor soon afterwards. I knew Gertrude still rode out, but rarely without her husband... had her ardour cooled, towards her shameless lover? In truth I'd thought little about it, being busy with my playfellow the Prince. I seized the cup and took a restoring pull.

'Nothing passed,' I told her. 'I sang for him when he was here, and that's all.'

'I heard he got you to spin a dirty rhyme, and displeased Her Highness.'

'That was for the Prince - and besides, the King allowed it.'

'It's said they didn't speak again after that night, the King and his brother. They hate each other, don't they?'

'You listen to too much gossip,' I told her. 'It's not worth a turd, dwelling on the affairs of high-born folk. Best keep your eyes down, do your work and take what pleasures you can.'

'That's easy to say when you're a royal fool, Yorick. It seems to me you do well enough out of high-born folk's business.'

'This grows tedious,' I said. 'Are you game for more frolicking, or not?'

'Why does Thura dislike you so?' Gunhild asked. And when I hesitated: 'She spreads bad things about you.'

'What sort of things?' I asked, uneasily.

'She said your mother was mad, and you'll end up the same.'

'Do you believe her?'

'How can I know what to think? The way you are sometimes - like when you wake up shouting in the night. Folk have heard you.'

I gave no answer; I had no desire to speak of the *mareridt*.

'And when you cavort with the Prince... leaping about, pretending to be an animal and such. Next you'll be howling at the moon, like the wolf-boy we had in my village. The men drove him out in the end, with pitchforks.'

'I make Prince Hamlet laugh,' I said, 'as I make you laugh.'

'You used to, when I first came here,' Gunhild said. 'Now you barely trouble yourself. Just mumble a gibe or two, while you get my dugs out.'

Yorick was silent after that. He knew the signs: Gunhild was tiring of him. Mayhap she'd even had a notion he might prove a fitting husband, before deciding that he wouldn't. Nor, for his part, was Yorick eager for a wife... not since Runa was taken from him.

'I'm an arrant knave,' I said. 'And it's late... you'd best go to your own bed.'

Which she did, soon after; nor did she share mine again.

By wintertime, when Hamlet and I rarely ventured outdoors save to the warmth of the stables, there was no denying that we were Boon Companions, as I'd hoped from the time when I first saw him. He would greet me eagerly once he was released from Rathulf's charge, and demand I be his horse again, or his bloodhound: I did a fair performance as a tracking-dog, snuffling about the floors for a scent. With the Prince on my back I would then bound off through the palace corridors, sometimes stopping in the kitchens for a mug. Though the welcomes we received after our first visits had lessened somewhat: Thura's forbidding looks were enough to keep the maids at their tasks.

In truth, what Gunhild had told me in the summer troubled me somewhat, about Thura's spreading of hurtful rumours. Then, she had always done so, it seemed, though I could barely recall the cause; the maids I'd bedded seemed to mingle together now, in one great cauldron of lustful memories. From Gunhild, I had moved on with trying to turn the fair Yiva's dislike of me into something more promising. There had been no progress, yet I remained hopeful, being so lifted by my new status as Prince's Fool; in truth, I see now that I was indeed *puffed up*, as Thura had once called me. And yet...

And yet: I was not so puffed up that, when Prince Hamlet raised the matter of my joining him at his lessons, I would seize it like a hound does a bone.

'By the gods, Highness, what can you be thinking?' I asked. 'Such things are for noble folk like you, not for a servant like me.'

'I'm lonely in the schoolroom with just Rathulf,' the Prince said. 'I wish for a playfellow... we could make up rhymes about him.'

'He would be most displeased by that,' I said. 'As would the King and Queen. Besides, they would never allow me to be taught as you are.'

'Why should they not?' Hamlet countered, putting on his stubborn look - a trait of his which had begun to appear of late. Indeed, as his fifth birthday drew close it was noticed how he had grown in sureness as well as in stature. Then, he was Gertrude's child, and *gammelklog*... a notion which at times gave me cause for unease.

'Because you're a prince, Highness, and will rule someday,' I told him. 'There's much you have to learn, of which I've no need.'

'Would you not like to read?' Hamlet asked. 'I can read a lot of words already. And soon I'll be able to write more than *dog* and *man* and the like - I could send you messages, and you could read them yourself.'

'Indeed, yet it's... it's unseemly,' I said, surprised to find myself sounding like Rathulf. 'I swear, Her Highness the Queen would not wish you to have lessons with me.'

'My father the King might,' Hamlet said. 'He listens to me when I talk – unlike the Queen. She's cold towards me at times, Yorick... I know not why.'

I looked away then; his speech was moving in a direction that troubled me. We were in the High Hall, which was deserted that afternoon. The King was hosting ambassadors in the presence chamber, while Gertrude was closeted with her ladies.

'I could ask Mattheus to speak to him,' the Prince said, brightening on a sudden.

I gulped. 'The priest? Why so – I mean, why would he?'

'Because he's kind and good,' came the answer.

'But, Highness...' I struggled to marshal my argument. 'Folk don't go to school at my age – I'm a man, without the appetite for learning that you have. And I have duties to perform, like entertaining the King.'

'When did you last do so?' Hamlet demanded, in a tone of triumph. 'Besides, you have naught to busy you in the mornings... they say you lie abed 'til noon.'

'It's false,' I lied. 'I'm up with the skylarks... I merely keep to myself.'

'I could order you to serve me, even at my lessons,' the Prince said.

'You could, Highness,' I replied - and now it struck me that he would get his way in this matter. The notion dismayed me... and yet, did it not excite me too? On a sudden I had a picture of the young Gertrude, haughty and impatient as she spoke of messages I couldn't read, and which would have to be spoken by Runa. Was there some part of Yorick – the scheming part – that wished to pay her for her contempt, and learn to read just to spite her?

'I will ask Mattheus,' Hamlet said, nodding firmly. 'And he will ask my father if you can be a scholar like me.' Before I could reply he turned and clambered on to a stool, then up on the High Table itself.

'Now catch me when I jump off,' he ordered. 'When you do, I'll give you a kiss.'

I caught him, and was rewarded with a kiss on the lips.

And thereafter winter gave way to a cold spring, and Hamlet was five years old, and for the first time in his life Yorick found himself in the chapel, face to face with pious Mattheus.

It was not of my choosing. The invitation, as Mattheus called it – though to Yorick's mind it was an order like any other – was for a short meeting, whereby the priest might speak of certain matters touching on Prince Hamlet. Hence, on a cloudy morning, with a mix of resentment and foreboding, the Prince's Fool slouched to the chapel and pushed open the doors, to enter a cool and silent interior heavy with the scent of incense. And there was Mattheus, holding out his hands.

'Master Yorick, welcome. Will you sit with me?' He gestured to the front pews, where we sat down a little way apart.

'I thought it was time we talked, you and I,' Mattheus said, observing my unease with a faint smile. 'You're a man who keeps his distance, I see.'

I made no answer, at which his smile faded to be replaced by a look of concern.

'I'm not your enemy,' he murmured. 'I could even be your friend.'

'With a deep-dyed sinner like me?' I countered. 'Why trouble yourself?'

'It's no trouble... and to bring just one sinner to repentance is its own reward.'

'I hear you forgo the company of women,' I said, to embarrass him. 'Was it advice you wanted, on how to split the whisker?'

He drew a breath. 'You've no cause for anger, Yorick. I asked you to come because we share a love and concern for Prince Hamlet. He has spoken of you to me, and-'

'It's a mad notion, me going to school,' I said, cutting him short. 'I've neither the wit nor the will. He's a child. In a few days he'll have forgotten about it, and clamour for something else. More, the Queen will never allow it, so...'

'How can you be sure of that?' Matteus broke in.

'Because I've known her since she too was a child, as I've learned to know my place.'

He paused a while, then: 'Have you truly - learned your place, I mean? From what I can see, you're the most restless soul in Helsingor.'

'Is that why you called me in?' I asked with a sneer. 'To save my maggoty soul? Best to admit defeat there, I'd say.'

He closed his eyes; was he praying? I wondered - then came a shock.

'It's been suggested to me that you're possessed,' Mattheus said, opening his eyes wide. 'There are some who believe I should carry out an exorcism – cast out the unclean spirits you harbour. That, or they would have you cast out of the King's service instead.'

I gaped. 'What – me, occupied by demons? Are you in earnest?'

'There are some who have suggested it,' he corrected.

'Like who?' I gave a start. 'The Queen?'

A kindly smile appeared, which set Yorick on edge. He might have blurted some choice crudity, but was forestalled. 'Peace - I'm not among them,' Mattheus said mildly. 'I see an unhappy man, who could be a deal more than he is.'

'A pox on you,' I threw back. 'You know naught of me. And I thought it was the Prince we were here to talk of.'

'Well then, let's do so,' Mattheus said, somewhat brisk on a sudden. 'He asks me to speak to the King for you, about your being his schoolfellow and sharing his lessons. Most men would deem it an honour, not to say a rare privilege, to study their letters. Yet you shy from it... why is that, I wonder?'

'I've told you, I'm a fool and a clod. Ask anyone hereabouts.'

'I pray you, don't do that,' Mattheus said, with a trace of a frown. 'Talk to me as if I were a simpleton, I mean. Nor are you, whatever you claim.'

I met his eye; perhaps he wasn't such a whoreson worm after all, I thought. And Hamlet liked him well enough...

'See now, I'd do anything to please the Prince,' I said. 'He's like a son to me - he brightens my life. But going to school with him? That's, well...'

'Is it his tutor you dislike?' Matheus enquired. 'Is that the true reason for your unwillingness?'

'I'd be a sore trial to Corambis – I mean Rathulf,' I told him. 'And why are you so eager that I agree? What matters it to you if I learn to read or not?'

'Since you ask me, I'll give you fair answer,' Mattheus said. 'I believe it would be good for His Highness to have your company. Two often learn better than one, in my experience. You could even challenge the tutor, with your ready wit. He proposes to teach the Prince rhetoric - but how can a boy learn to debate well, with only the learned Rathulf as his adversary?' He paused, then: 'In truth, to my eyes he's more suited to being a counsellor, akin to Lord Huginn. Perhaps that will be his destiny one day...' a wan smile appeared. 'There now,' he added. 'I've spoken my mind, and likely provided fare for the gossips... perhaps we have that much in common, at the least.'

Confiteo: I was taken aback. So, it wasn't just Yorick who thought Rathulf a prating bellows, even if he did have a wife? I must have allowed a grin to slip out, at which Mattheus's smile broadened – and now I knew I was losing the battle; likely I'd lost it before I even entered the chapel.

'A Prince needs to acquire more than mere knowledge,' Mattheus said. 'He needs insight, and the power to reason for himself - that way, he may be brought to greatness.' He eyed me for a moment, then: 'Will you be other than merely his jester? Will you be his helpmate too, in more than mere frolics?'

Yorick sighed, opened and closed his mouth - and submitted; abased himself even, or so it appeared to him then. Though I was afraid and not a little ashamed: afraid that Rathulf would make my life one of misery and humiliation, and ashamed that I hadn't the means to fight back. I might have longed for my stable-lad days, when I would settle a dispute with my fists - or for my time with the players, when between us we could face the world and laugh at it. But here was another turning I had never compassed... had the hex Edela seen it? Was this one more thing she had chosen not to tell me?

One thing I knew: for all her wild and ragged ways, Gitte would have been awed to see Yorick raised from fool to scholar, as perhaps would Makan. And when all was said and sifted, it was the Prince's wish.

Those thoughts weighed upon me in the days after, until another event drove them from my mind. For hard upon my talk with pious Mattheus, followed one I dreaded.

I was called before the King, to attend him in close conference.

TWENTY

King Hamlet had changed, after his first years of marriage to Gertrude; there was no denying it, though none spoke of it. The mighty sea rover had passed from ardent suitor to fawning bridegroom to devoted husband – and now? King of Denmark, certainly; scourge of his enemies, without doubt; father to a prince... and wife to a queen who mocked him behind his back, and had cuckolded him with his own brother. The last was known to only two people at Helsingor, and Yorick was one of them: a notion that at times awed him, and at others froze his bones. Such thoughts were seldom far from his mind, most especially on that afternoon when he was brought to the King, well-scrubbed and clad in his best attire, to make his bow and wait.

His Highness was not alone: there was Huginn, with his staff and his belly – have I spoken of how fat he'd grown, by that time? There were attendants too, of the sort the King favoured: tall and alert, armed as if for battle at any moment. On a table, charts and maps were spread out as if some new campaign were being planned. At sight of me, however, the King moved to his throne and sat – not in his new chair but on Rorik's old throne, where I had last seen Gertrude. To my relief the Queen was not present... it would be manly talk. Yorik drew himself to full height and tried to look martial.

'You know why I've summoned you,' Hamlet said.

'I believe so, Highness... does it touch on the Prince's schooling?'

He gave a nod, then: 'I find myself in a dilemma, *Hofnar* - betwixt satisfying my son's desires, and those of his mother. The Queen thinks you will be a distraction to Prince Hamlet during his lessons - as does his tutor.'

'As do I,' Huginn chimed in... and was it my fancy, but did a look of annoyance flicker across his master's features?

'And yet, the priest counsels me that it would suit the Prince to have you there,' the King continued, as if he hadn't heard. 'Though I'm uncertain of it. Hamlet reads quite well already, while you would lag so far behind him, you could hamper his progress. What say you?'

'Only that I would try not to, sire,' I answered. 'I wish only what's best for His Highness.'

'What's best for him is for others to decide,' Huginn said. 'It appears to me you've forgotten your place of late, *Hofnar*. You act more like the Prince's confidant than his fool.'

Yorick lowered his eyes; it would have been unwise to betray his thoughts, which just then involved kicking the chamberlain's staff away and putting him down on his fat arse. Whereupon, to my surprise, the King turned to Huginn and spoke an order that startled him.

'I beg pardon, Highness?'

'I said leave us. I would speak with Yorick alone.'

'But sire, I understood... that is...'

He struggled to find the words, and Yorick knew why: he was still Gertrude's man at Court, charged with reporting anything that was said outside her hearing. Yet when I looked at the King, my spirits lifted: this time he would brook no refusal. He merely waited with raised eyebrows, until at last his chamberlain bowed and turned to go. Though as he left, he threw a swift glance at me in which I read the warning: *one word out of place, and you're finished.*

'I'll admit one thing,' the elder Hamlet said once we were alone, his guards having moved discreetly aside. 'My son is cheerful when he's with you. He loves you, almost as a father.' And when I flinched a little: 'Moreover, I like what he tells me... how you sport with him in rough fashion. A boy should be able to run and leap without fear, to climb trees and to bowl and throw quoits... those are worthy pursuits, befitting one who will learn soldierly skills.'

Now Yorick was taken aback. Having expected some rebuff, he was garnering praise instead. Would it last? he wondered. Where was the sting?

'As I've said, the Queen is of a different opinion,' the King went on. 'When she first spoke of our son enjoying such pleasures as were denied to her when she was a child, I believe she had other things in mind than his sharing crude jests with stablemen, not to say fishing and chasing rabbits. I even hear you and he had a battle with rotten fruit, which resulted in a ruined pair of breeches. Is that so?'

Yorick admitted that it was. And though he was reminded of an occasion in the High Hall when the King himself had permitted Yorick to be pelted to the ruin of more than a pair of breeches, he kept silent on the matter.

'Well...' His Highness eyed me, until I grew uneasy; the terrible secret I held was so stark in my mind, I could almost see it: a dark cloud that threatened to burst asunder – and at what followed, I went rigid.

'What are they saying, out there?' Hamlet asked, with a jerk of his head towards the doors.

Confiteo: I was confounded. He used the very words King Rorik had spoken to me, a long time ago. Rorik had demanded the truth and nothing less - but here and now, the truth was the very last thing Yorick could speak. I coughed, then:

'About what, Highness?'

'About the Prince, of course,' came the answer, to my immense relief. 'Is he admired by the common folk? Is he deemed courageous? Has he a ready wit? Come, you're closer to him than most – I might even say than his own father.'

'Highness, surely not,' I gulped. 'He is indeed loved and admired, as he is quick-witted and brave – and unwavering in his affection for you. He delights in hearing your tales of war and valour. He's a prince in every respect – and a great credit to his royal father.'

Whereupon, with heart pounding, I dropped my gaze and prayed silently that he would shift his speech towards another topic.

'Well, that's pleasing enough.'

The King paused, then assumed his dour look that would once have made me wary, but was now a comfort. 'Then, that's your skill, is it not?' He said. 'To spout stuff that pleases, and so divert a monarch from his cares?'

'True enough, Highness,' I answered. 'I was brought up to do little else.'

'Which seems a waste, to me,' Hamlet said. 'You might have been a soldier. Do you yourself not believe that?'

'I, sire?' I tried my humble look, but somehow it failed. 'Now it's you who flatter, if I dare put it so. I'm a baseborn fellow - to some, little more than a beggar.'

'A beggar who sports with a prince, and would be his schoolfellow too.'

With mingled feelings, I waited: from a notion that the King would reject the madcap notion of Yorick joining Hamlet at his lessons, I saw now that the opposite was likely. I might have made reply, but had no stomach for it – and what confounded me most was seeing that Gertrude's husband would go against her wishes. Was he no longer the compliant man he had been, ready to indulge her every wish? The answer came, and soon enough.

'So be it, then,' the King said. 'You may attend Hamlet at his lessons. If his tutor protests, tell him his father has decided it would benefit him to study alongside a companion. I hope you'll use the time well – now, is there aught you wish to say?'

There was nothing. And soon afterwards I was dismissed, finding myself outside the doors - where Huginn awaited me, boiling with quiet fury.

'You've gone too far, Yorick,' he breathed, moving so close to me that we almost touched. 'I've warned you often enough, and now you stand on the edge. Be assured that henceforth, everything you say and do will be observed and weighed. Now get yourself gone – and remember.'

Yorick remembered, for a week or two; but after that, once he found his daily lessons with Prince Hamlet somewhat different to what he expected, he as good as forgot. He was set on a perilous course, which would lead to the sorry case he's in now, but he was too easily diverted to take heed of looming danger. *Lege*, Gentle Reader, and beware: it's not pride that goeth before a fall, but carelessness – and Yorick, who now spent so much of the day in the company of his beloved master, was Carelessness in person, as in some old play: the kind of character who struts on to the stage and promptly falls on his arse.

And from the start, there was the troublesome presence of that other arse: Rathulf, or Corambis as we now called him.

To begin with, to say that Yorick was adrift *sans* lodestone would be short of the mark: he was a dolt of the first degree, whose tutor made no secret of scorning him for it. While Hamlet made quick progress, reading aloud with Corambis, Yorick was left with a child's hornbook, muttering oaths while attempting to puzzle out the shapes on it. By the end of the first week he knew the letters of the alphabet, though how they fitted together to make words was a mystery. It was the Prince who came to my rescue, demanding that our tutor explain.

'In truth, Highness, I cannot help but feel the task is beyond me,' Corambis said, forcing a smile that merely conveyed weariness. 'Master Yorick's mind moves along paths already well-trodden, of which I've small knowledge.' He shifted his gaze to me. 'How he expects me to fulfil this duty he's contrived to burden me with, I'm at a loss to know.'

'Well, you're the wise man and I'm the fool,' I said. 'If you don't know, how should I?'

He sighed, tugging at his beard which already showed flecks of grey; recalling Mattheus's words, I could indeed see him as a chamberlain, if one without Huginn's cruel streak. In truth, there's no great harm in Corambis, save his dullness... and his sickly smiles, and his high-sounding words. 'You are my *vexator*, Yorick,' he once said. 'Some say that every tutor needs one.'

'Let us go over the letters, then,' he said that day, bending over me where I sat. 'As I speak them, you will follow. Try to make a picture for each one. *Videlicet*, A... what does it resemble to you?'

'A pointed arch?' I suggested.

'Perhaps... A for arch.' He peered at me. 'And B?'

'An arse, if you turn it on its side.' I showed him. 'See the buttocks? B for buttocks.'

At which Hamlet let out a howl of laughter, with which Yorick, of course, could not help but join. And though I recovered sooner than did the Prince, it was too late: angered, Corambis stood up and stepped away.

'If this is how it will be, then I'm powerless to aid you,' he snorted. 'Henceforth I'll leave you to master each letter as you choose. When you can understand a few simple words, call on me and we will read together. As for writing...' he shook his head. 'That, you will find, is a great deal harder. Now, with your leave, Highness...' He turned to Hamlet. 'Would you care to go to your dinner? I know I would.'

So the lesson ended, and school was dismissed. And yet that afternoon, walking with Hamlet in the garden, I found myself the target of his reproach.

'I don't like it when you mock him, Yorick,' the Prince said, after a short silence. 'Even if you make me laugh. He was hurt... he desires only to teach us.'

'To teach you, Highness,' I answered. 'I'm a trial to him - I knew it would be so. I tried to counsel you against it.'

'But I thought you wanted to read, as I do. And to write things.'

I sought for an answer, but had none. It was a fine day, summer was upon us, and in truth I feared that, now I was at study with Hamlet, our afternoons together might lack their old excitement. The Prince was somewhat subdued, I saw, and hence it was my task to lift his humour.

'I could have done a great fart this morning,' I told him. 'But I held it in - I feared I would inflate like a bladder. That shows I care for Master Corambis, does it not? I'd no wish to poison him.'

But he barely smiled. He was carrying a switch I'd cut from a hedgerow, swishing it through the grass. He stopped and faced me.

'Do you ever fall into melancholy, Yorick?'

'I, Highness?' I put on my horrified look. 'I dare not – what use is a jester who's miserable?'

'Now you mock me,' he answered. 'I grow tired of people who think me dull-witted, merely because I'm little. The Queen mocks me at times... she says odd things. When I ask what she means, she says I wouldn't understand.'

I was silent; from wishing to divert him, I now thought to let him unburden himself.

'There's a Latin word – *ignominia*,' Hamlet said. 'It means "shame". I've heard her say it in Confession, with Mattheus. She has shame, though I don't know why.'

'You hear her during Confession?' I asked in surprise. 'But that's told in secret, to the priest.'

'I creep to the curtain and listen,' the Prince said. 'I have very good hearing.'

'I know, Highness, but should you eavesdrop like that? I think the Queen would be angry if she knew.'

He thought for a moment, then: 'She has secrets, unbeknownst to my father.'

Yorick stiffened.

'She talks privately with her new maid, Yiva.'

'Yiva? I thought she was yet in the kitchens.'

'She's been taken from there,' Hamlet informed me. 'She's too fair and too clever, the Queen says. And she can sew... they sit close together.'

'And you eavesdrop... I mean, you overhear them?'

'Sometimes, before the Queen sends me off to play. She wants me to learn the lute, she says, but my father does not. He will have me learn to shoot a bow and to fence. When I'm older and can ride well enough, I must tilt at the quintain.'

'And is that your desire, too?'

Hamlet considered. 'I think I should rather be a scholar, like Corambis.' He looked up. 'In truth, I no longer like that name we gave him, Yorick. But nor do I like Rathulf, which is coarse. I would like to find another.'

'Well, you can if you choose,' Yorick allowed, busy thinking on what he'd said.

'His father was a Pole, Lord Huginn says - so mayhap he should be named Polonius. I will ask the King what he thinks.'

Startled, I regarded him. 'You're full of invention, Highness,' I said.

And yet the name stuck, and it does still.

Thereafter, in the year that followed, the ground beneath Yorick's feet shifted almost before he noticed it. From those early weeks of mocking the hapless Corambis-turned-

Polonius as a prating pedant, he was surprised to find himself becoming drawn to his studies - even looking forward to them. *Confiteo:* I dislike the old Yorick now; that ragged rogue with his jokes about farting and fucking, who found himself shamed by a six-year-old boy. A boy who could read Latin verse, and write whole passages in a fair hand, and count without using a box of beads. A boy who began to dispute in advance of one of his years – to the greater shame of Yorick, who could only pen simple phrases. And yet, in his new role as scholar-jester, Yorick became absorbed as he had never imagined. Letters that had appeared but marks began to have a life, joining together to make whole words and at last whole sentences... and it was then that he began to see everything with a fresh eye.

How proud my mother would have been, I realised, and my almost-father too. Here was a world of which they had no knowledge – nor expected to have, nor even desired. How the turnabout would have amazed them: the baseborn son of Gitte the Three-fingered and Makan the jester being able to read aloud... there were times when even I disbelieved it. Yet it was true: by the end of the following winter, having worked harder at anything I'd done since I toiled in the stables, I had stepped out of the gloom of ignorance into sunshine. *Ecce aurora*!

I learned many new words. I could read and I could write a little, and I was improving fast at both. And though I might thank whatever gods there be that I have the skill now to tell my tale by myself, it has come at a price: it was my downfall, even if I was too blind to see it. And though there was one who did, I was too stuffed with my own bombast to understand, until it was too late.

But let me tell of it now: tell of Mattheus, and how he tried to catch me as I fell.

TWENTY-ONE

It began with a prayer-book.

Spring was come again, and I'd kept clear of both priest and chapel since that day Mattheus had persuaded me to attend Prince Hamlet at his lessons. Yet now my case was altered, since it was known throughout Helsingor that Yorick was a man who could read messages - not that any ever came his way. Instead he found himself viewed with suspicion by everyone, from the chamberlain down to the kitchen-maids. Even Gunhild shunned me, while Thura, of course, continued to regard me as a rogue who should have been flogged at birth. What with Huginn shunning me whenever he saw me, and the King often away fortress-visiting, and Gertrude always out of sight – which in truth, caused me more unease than if she'd called me in to chastise me – I began to think I'd barely a foe to call my own, let alone a friend. Apart from my beloved Hamlet, that is, who was pleased with the progress of his overgrown schoolfellow. Yet even the Prince was withdrawn at times, seemingly talking to himself, so that it grew somewhat harder to amuse him. I began to be troubled by his silences, and decided one day to draw him out of his humours.

We had been studying an old play that morning, and though I knew only a few words of Latin, culled from Polonius's spoutings, I found its substance most satisfying. It was writ by a Roman called Plautus, about a slave who's cleverer than his master and shows him up for the clod he is. It tickled Yorick a good deal, and fitted a fancy of his about turning tables on his betters – but Hamlet was less fond.

'I would have noble sagas, about emperors and kings,' he said. 'It's easy to mock... the world's more suited to melancholy, I think. I see enough of it here at Helsingor - *ergo*, why should it be different elsewhere?'

How *gammelklog* he was become! 'But it is, Highness,' I assured him. 'Not that I've travelled anywhere, but I've known men who have.' And on a whim, I began to tell him of my playing days, when I lived with Eghil and Sveinn and the others, and Jofurr the serpent.

Hamlet was intrigued. 'Where are the player-folk now?' He asked. 'Did my grandfather send them away? Why do they not come here?'

'There was little call for them, so they chose to leave Denmark. I know not where they are; perhaps they'll come again one day.'

'They should – they must.' The Prince considered, then: 'I'll ask the King. If he will not send for them, then when I'm King, I will do so.'

'That's a fine idea. If I'm still here, I would be most happy to see them again.'

'If you're still here?' Hamlet frowned. 'Why should you not be? You wouldn't go away as the players did, would you?'

'No – never. Yet I'm older than you... a lot may happen in the years ahead.'

'But you make me laugh,' he protested, 'when no-one else does.'

'Then, why not command me?' I said, as an amusing memory sprang to mind. 'Order me to outlive you - on pain of death!'

He regarded me solemnly, then sighed. 'You're an odd fellow, Yorick.'

'The odds are that I am indeed odd,' I said. 'But it's we oddballs who in secret rule the world, as Master Plautus shows us in his play.'

'Mattheus thinks you should be baptised,' Hamlet said.

I stared at him. 'When did he say that?'

'He counsels the Queen, often. They talk about sin a good deal.'

Well they might, thought Yorick. But to the Prince he said: 'I've no wish to be baptised, Highness. I'm an unworthy fool - a *scurra*, as our tutor would say.'

'You're mistaken. Polonius says you're cleverer than he thought... a quick learner, he says. I think you make him uncomfortable.'

'Weary, more like,' I said. But it was I who was discomfited, the conversation having moved in ways I hadn't foreseen.

'Mayhap you should leave off studying,' Hamlet said, his eyes on the ground.

Well, *confiteo*: I was aghast. 'Is that your wish, Highness?' I enquired, struggling to collect myself. 'Do I distract you, as it was once feared I would?'

'It's your distractions I love,' he said, looking up. 'With you I may do as I please and speak as I please, but not in the schoolroom. There I must learn, and strive to be wise - as Huginn say, or even as Mattheus. He's the wisest of all.'

'But I was ordered to study with you, by the King himself,' I said forlornly. 'To quit the schoolroom would be to disobey him.'

'I will ask him what he wishes, when he returns home,' Hamlet said. 'Will you speak with Mattheus? I believe he would comfort you.'

I was silent; a great loneliness seemed to be enfolding me. Was even my beloved playfellow spurning me now? I sought for some reply, but all I could do was nod.

And only a few days later, an order came from the King: Yorick was no longer required to attend Prince Hamlet at his lessons. He might continue to provide sport and exercise, at times of the Prince's choosing, but since his tutor now wished to advance his studies – debating in Latin, and so forth - then the fool's presence in the schoolroom would merely be a bridle, to hold him back.

That night, Yorick retired to his chamber with a jug of ale stolen from the brewing-house and drank himself to sleep. And in the morning, drowsy and morose, he received another order that did nothing to lift his spirits: he was to go to the chapel and seek Father Mattheus, who was eager to speak with him.

'I have a gift for you, Master Yorick,' the priest said.

He held out a small book, bound in good leather. Yorick gazed at it through bleared eyes, but did not take it.

'It's a book of prayer,' Mattheus informed me. 'Now that you can read, I pray you'll receive it with my blessing.

Indeed,' he went on, seeing my reluctance, 'it could be that this was destined. It should be a comfort to you... and I would be glad to answer any questions you have regarding what's within. More, I could help you to read better, now that you no longer take lessons from the Prince's tutor. Does this please you?'

'Which answer shall I give?' I muttered, glowering; I had an urge to knock his book of prayer to the floor. 'The one you expect: that I'm honoured, and will go away at once to read with diligence? Or the one that comes from my dark heart?'

A pause, then: 'I would never wish any man to speak, other than from his heart.'

'In that case, you can take your precious book and plug your arsehole with it.'

He did that habit of his – closing his eyes, taking a breath and then opening them wider than before. 'I had a notion you might say something to that effect,' he murmured.

'You're a clever one, right enough,' I replied.

'I told you once before, Yorick, I'm not your enemy.'

'I'm most relieved, for I've got enough of those.'

'Why do you use me in this fashion?' He asked. 'Am I a mere target for your anger? Do you expect me to turn the other cheek, as our Saviour did, and invite further insult?'

'Is that not your wish?' I retorted. 'Isn't martyrdom your chief aim?'

'No – my aim is to help you, if I can.'

'Indeed?' I pretended to ponder the matter. 'Then, what if I ask you to cease trying to turn me into the sort of pious fool who falls to his knees every day, and leave me to my own devices?'

'And what are those, pray - your devices?'

'Fooling and fucking would be among them,' I told him. 'And drinking, when I get the chance. And jesting with stablemen, and bating that whoreson gravedigger who thinks himself such a wit. And waiting on the King to call on me, even if he never does.'

'It sounds a somewhat empty life to me,' Mattheus observed.

I made no answer; but in truth my anger was ebbing somewhat. There was no great harm in him, even though in the dullness race I thought him a forerunner alongside Polonius. Sensing my demeanour, he held out the prayer-book again.

'Will you take it anyway?' He asked. 'For my sake, if no other?'

Whereupon I sighed and took it, thinking it would at the least spare me a sermon - but he wasn't done yet.

'The Queen is troubled when her mind alights on you, Yorick.'

I stiffened.

'She believes you draw Prince Hamlet to rascally ways and improper speech. He is of royal blood, and should be served as befits one destined to rule.'

I gave a start. 'Was it you who put the notion in his head, to speak with the King and have me forbidden to study with the Prince?'

'It was not,' Mattheus said firmly. 'I bear you no ill-will... why do you persist in mistrusting me?'

'Then it was the Queen,' I said, barely listening. 'She would have me cast out... I wonder she hasn't done so already. Save that Hamlet is my friend...'

I broke off: he was looking hard at me, though seemingly without malice. 'Why would she do so?' he asked. 'Indeed, why do you think she dislikes you?'

I hesitated, then throwing all caution – nay, all good sense – aside, I met his eye.

'I thought you might know why, being her confessor.'

He fell silent. I had perplexed him, and at once I rued my reckless words. Mattheus was - he is – no more than a year or two older than me, yet we are as light and dark. If he'd been of a different stamp, I thought, willing to share a jug and frolic with a couple of maids, how different our case would have been; but that was chaff in the wind.

'What passes in the confessional is sacred, and not to be repeated outside,' he said.

'I know that,' I said.

'Yet I may tell you what has *not* passed,' Mattheus added sharply. 'I have never heard a word spoken against you by the Queen... indeed, she never talks of you at all, save in chance conversation. At those times she expresses only regret... regret that you are falling from debauchery into madness. In short, she fears for your soul.'

Confiteo: here was a shock. I'd no cause to doubt his words, in which case... on a sudden I recalled Hamlet's talk of *ignominia* – the shame the Queen was prey to, as he thought. It had come to me that she would have confessed her sin to Mattheus: the sin of cuckolding her husband with his brother – yet now I doubted it. Instead she hid those deeds, to which Yorick was a party if not a witness...

I tried to keep expression from my face. 'So - it was she who told you I was possessed.' And when his silence was answer enough: 'I believe I asked you before,' I said. 'Now I ask again – do you believe it?'

He hesitated, then: 'As I told you, I see a troubled man.'

'Yet, not one who harbours evil?'

'I think not,' came the answer, albeit after another pause.

'Then, a pox on those that do,' I said. 'And for your sake I'll try to read the book. But I'll not come to chapel, even if the Queen does fear for my soul.'

I began to rise, but once again Mattheus stayed me.

'I'm told you once had dealings with a hex, who was cast out and lived apart,' he said, gently. 'I've even heard it said she bewitched you. Will you speak of her?' And before I could answer: 'Did she keep wild creatures as her familiars? A marten, say, or a fox?'

'She kept goats and hens,' I told him.

'Did you eat or drink anything, while you were in her company?'

'A cup of ale, once,' I answered, wary of these questions. 'It was a hot day.'

He considered, then: 'You have trod some dangerous paths, Yorick. I urge you to reflect upon your life. It's never too late for a man to change himself.'

'Might I go now?' I asked, to which he merely nodded. Whereupon I left, walking more quickly than I intended.

Confiteo: I never did read his prayer-book.

Some days later, Huginn the chamberlain was strolling in the courtyard after taking supper with the Queen and the Prince. Mayhap he overdid himself at table, the gossips said; a surfeit of eels and pickled herrings was talked of, not to mention his putting away a whole pudding by himself. But others spoke of something else: harsh words spoken between Huginn and the Queen, at which young Hamlet was sent out of the High Hall. At the end of their discourse Gertrude had swept angrily away, with her maids hurrying to keep up: a common enough sight in the Queen's youth. Huginn had sat alone for a while before taking himself outdoors – and it was there that he fell.

It was dark, and some time passed before he was discovered, lying on his back like a bloated beetle. Sentries arrived, he was carried to his chamber and laid upon his bed, and the King's physician summoned. But by morning it was clear that nothing could be done: pale as milk, unable to rise or even to speak except to complain of great pains in his stomach, the chamberlain died with only Mattheus in attendance along with a servant or two. And in truth, few were much troubled by the news save Gertrude, who made a great show of grief and called for a time of mourning. As for Yorick…

Yorick walked in the King's garden, lifted his face to the sun and breathed the heady air of relief. With Huginn's passing a weight was lifted, and he could only thank the gods for his good fortune. Until, that is, the morning of the funeral came, and along with everyone else he was obliged to stand by the graveside and look solemn while Mattheus did his office, commending our beloved brother Huginn's spirit into the hands of his Lord.

The King was absent on some business, but Gertrude was present. It was the first time I had seen her in a long while, but she was some way off and veiled; I doubt she even noticed me. Throughout the ceremony, in the hallowed plot reserved for kings and nobles, she kept her head bowed until it was over, then retired indoors. The moment she was gone, people lost little time returning to their duties. Polonius saw me, and inclined his head stiffly as he went. Prince Hamlet was with him, and would have spoken to me had his tutor not ushered him inside; it seemed lessons would proceed as usual. So it was that, having nothing much to do, I found myself alone save for Absalom the son of Agnaar, plying his spade.

'You're the only one who's got a secure place here,' I told him. 'Seeing as there's always someone who'll need burying.'

'Me? I'm just a builder,' Absalom answered, in easy fashion. 'Yet the houses I make are the strongest, for they last 'til doomsday.'

'A pity that you won't,' I said; this promised to be an exchange of barbs for which I was more than ready, having been in good spirits since Huginn's death. 'What a loss that will be, to our common store of wit and invention.'

'I hear the Prince had you thrown out of school,' was his retort. 'Too dim-witted, were you? Or just soused, as usual?'

'I was glad of it,' I said. 'Being mewed up in that room with Polonius would drive any man to get soused.'

I had stepped closer to the grave, and peered over to view Huginn's portly body, wrapped in its winding sheet. 'Perhaps that's what did for our friend,' I said.

Absalom made no answer; merely threw a few shovelfuls on to the corpse in that steady way he had, while humming an air to himself. After a while, seeing I was in no hurry to move off, he turned and leaned on his spade.

'You're an idle rogue, Yorick. Then, when were you aught else?'

'I'm content just watching,' I said. 'Few men wield a spade with such skill as you.' Then, as he was about to speak, I got in first. 'Now's the moment you tell me you'll see me in the ground, isn't it? And how you'll spit in my grave?'

'I will,' he answered. 'And it may not be so far off. I hear you drink from morn 'til night… your guts must be pickled.'

'But not my wits,' I said. 'Even Huginn would admit that, if he could talk.'

He eyed me, then: 'That's not all he might say, if he could talk,' he muttered. 'For there's things not even you know,

Master Quick-tongue. A man in my place sees things others don't... nor would they wish to, I'd guess.'

'I'm intrigued,' I said. 'Will you share the fruits of your great knowledge?'

'Aye, mock!' Absalom threw back. 'That's all you're fit for, is it not? Poking fun at others - you've not done a day's work since they plucked you out of the stables.'

'True enough,' I said. 'Yet I'm in earnest. What is it Master Huginn might say, if he could talk? Come, you've caught my attention.'

'Have I so?' He scoffed. 'Why, do you think it must be about you?'

'Whether it is or no, will you not enlighten me?'

He hesitated, then shook his head. 'Nay, you'd mouth it all over Helsingor, and being the source of it, I'd be the one in trouble.' He turned his back and set to work again, but now he had pricked Yorick's curiosity.

'I can keep a secret,' I lied. 'Tell me, and I'll get you a flagon of Rhenish to cure your thirst.' And when he stopped working and turned: 'I swear it – even if I have to pay for it.'

'Step close, then,' he muttered after a moment. And when I did so: 'You never heard this from me, Yorick. If you spill it, I'll come for you... understand?'

I inclined my head, whereupon Absalom leaned on his spade and pointed downwards, to the half-covered body of Huginn.

'I saw him before he was shrouded,' he said, speaking low. 'And I've seen it before: that pallor... the blue lips. My father spoke of it once...' He looked away, then: 'He was poisoned. What with, I couldn't say – but that's what killed our friend the Chamberlain right enough: a noxious poison, and naught else.'

At which a chill stole about Yorick's vitals, which never truly went away again.

That same day he sold Mattheus's prayer-book for four *pennings* to the god-fearing stable-master, which paid not only for a jug of strong wine for Absalom, but another for himself. With which, clutching it to his body as though it were a pot of gold, he fled to his chamber, shoved everything he owned against the door and proceeded to drink himself into oblivion.

Thereafter I kept alone, in fear for my life.

TWENTY-TWO

It was clear as daylight: Gertrude wished me dead.

Of the two men at Helsingor who knew her secret, one had been poisoned, while the other was a lowly fool with no-one to protect him. It was the Queen who had contrived Huginn's death, of that I was certain; and if she could despatch the King's chamberlain with such ease, it would be a simple matter to send Yorick to the after-world too. If so, Absalom would have satisfaction sooner than even he expected. Not that Yorick would have dared to betray Gertrude, even if he could catch the ear of the King – but what if she was no longer sure of it? What if she'd decided to remove all risks of being found out? Or more likely, what if Lord Claudius wished it? It was well-known that I drank a good deal: perhaps, between the two of them, they had decided I could no longer be relied on to keep silent...

These were the thoughts that beset me as I hid myself away, creeping out only at night to steal food from the kitchens. I was become a creature of the dark, not even daring to have a light in the chamber. By day I dozed, waking only to listen at the door for footsteps, while the business of the castle went on below me. Sometimes I crouched by the window, trying to catch the speech of passers-by, but none came near enough. I heard riders, once a large party arriving in the courtyard which could have been the King returning from one of his forays. Otherwise, nothing; no-one sent for me, not even Prince Hamlet. It was that which troubled me the most, so that I began to wonder what he had been told. What rumours abounded, out there? That I was sick, even dying – if so, surely someone would come to look for me? Yet they did not; I was a ghost... and soon, other ghosts began to seek my company.

Makan came first, on a warm afternoon when I lay sweating on my pallet. I thought I was awake, sleep having eluded me for what seemed a long while... was I losing count of the days? All I know is that a kind of mist filled the room, and my almost-father appeared close by, wagging his finger.

'You failed again, Yorick,' he said. 'Your jests are stale... all that I taught you, gone to dust. You were a fellow of excellent fancy - now you slide into madness.'

'I don't,' I protested. 'You know me better than that.'

'Do you still have my shawm?' Makan asked. 'Why do you not play it?'

'I can't!' I wailed. 'What if I played the tabor instead? See, I can do it...'

I began to drum, hammering out a slow rhythm on my chest, but he was fading from sight. I tried to beat louder, but my arms were leaden. All I could manage was a feeble thud, then another - whereupon I awoke in a sweat, hearing loud knocking. With a shout I sat up – and knew it was no dream: there was someone at my door. Lurching from the bed, I stumbled towards it.

'Yorick?' A muffled voice called. 'Do you hear me? It's Father Mattheus.'

Mattheus... I sank to my knees, while more knocks came.

'Are you there? Yorick?'

'Here,' I croaked. 'I'm here...'

The latch went up and the door moved, then came up against the barricade of clothes, shoes and other stuffs I'd piled against it. Cursing under my breath I dragged them aside, then got to my feet as the door opened. There stood Mattheus, with a covered mug in his hand and a puzzled look on his face. In mingled distrust and relief, Yorick eyed him.

'I heard you were sick,' he said. 'The maids have sent you a posset.'

Dumbly, I stared at the mug.

'Why have you not sought help? The Prince is concerned – he asked me to seek you out.'

'A posset?' I muttered. 'Not wine, then.'

'Might I come in?'

I stood aside to let him enter. As he did so his nose wrinkled in distaste; he saw my tin pot, full of the emptyings of my bowels, and looked away.

'I wasn't expecting company,' I said, in surly fashion.

He gestured to the mug. 'Will you sit and drink this? It's milk, curdled with ale and sugar. There are herbs mixed in – one of the maids says it's a potion known to her family. It will cure anything, she swears.' He looked me over. 'Though how effective it is against mere drunkenness, I cannot say.'

'I'll taste it,' I growled, slumping on my bed. He handed me the posset, found the only stool, pulled it close and sat down.

'Best to drink while it's still warm,' he said.

I put aside the cloth that covered the mug and sniffed. I smelled spices, cloves and herb of rue. It was not what I needed, yet I thought to appease him before curtailing his visit; he was the last person I wanted to see. And my hands were shaky... trying to master them, I lifted the brew to my mouth, then froze.

'Which of the maids was it, who made this?' I asked.

Mattheus raised an eyebrow. 'I forget her name... does it matter?'

I made no answer; my mind was filled with sudden and furious fancies. He regarded me, and a frown appeared. 'What, do you think someone wishes to poison you?'

Again, I said nothing.

'Why would they? I fear your mind is playing tricks upon you, Yorick.'

Yet I could not bring myself to drink. My hands began to shake so much, he could not help but notice. 'Let me,' he said. And when I didn't understand, he reached out and took the mug. Regarding me over its rim, he took a sip.

'Pleasant enough,' he said. 'Will you not try it?'

I took it from him, and forced myself to drink.

'Good...' He smiled. 'Now, will you unburden yourself? You look as if you should.'

We talked then, for longer than I wanted; yet when all's said, his presence reassured me somewhat. I even finished the posset, which did no harm and may have eased my stomach. Mattheus listened and made no judgements, until I confessed to selling the prayer-book, which caused him some dismay.

'Well, at the least you placed it in good hands.' Somewhat briskly then, he began to speak of everyday matters – chief among which was that, following Huginn's sudden death, Polonius had been appointed Counsellor to the King.

'Then you were right in your prediction,' I said. 'But who tutors Prince Hamlet?'

'I do, for the present. Until some other may be found.'

Well now: a glimmer of hope had arrived, that I might persuade him to petition the King to let me return to my lessons – until I recalled that it was Hamlet himself who had raised doubts about my presence.

'Will you convey my love and devotion to His Highness the Prince?' I asked. 'Tell him I've been unwell, but am eager to be up and sporting with him again?'

But to that, I received no ready answer. Mattheus paused, then: 'The Queen has asked me to convey her wishes for your recovery.'

I put on my blandest look.

'Her Highness also suggested that you should take such time as you need, to restore yourself to good health,' he went on. 'While you remain here, someone will be ordered to bring you food and drink... though not wine. Weak ale or milk is recommended.'

I lowered my gaze; his meaning was plain enough. Doubtless he had been told that Makan drank himself to death... was Yorick expected to follow?

'There's no necessity,' I said. 'I'll rise and go about, and see what-'

'I would advise against it, just now,' Mattheus interrupted.

I looked up sharply. 'You advise?'

'The Queen feels that you need time to reflect. Rest, and cleanse your body of those things which have enfeebled it - and read, too,' he added. 'I'll have a bible brought to you. It's a matter of great joy to me, that you're now able to read the words of God.'

'Are you telling me I'm confined here?' I asked in alarm. 'That I'm a prisoner?'

'Of course not. You are an invalid, who wants care and rest.'

'I do not - I want some air.'

'In time, yes...' Mattheus looked kindly at me. 'Put aside the Queen's thoughts if you must, and be advised by me. Show willing... keep apart, read the holy book, and allow Her Highness to forget. When you emerge, fresh and...'

'Sober?' I broke in, to which his silence was answer enough. I drew breath, my mind busy again. 'I'll stay here 'til the morrow,' I said. 'Then if I'm well...' but a frown was coming on. 'You say I'm not a prisoner? That I can walk out of the door when I choose?'

'There's no lock, is there?'

There was not – nor is there still, I might add; yet to say I was uneasy would be short of the mark. I needed to be left alone then, and to think.

'Well, I thank you,' I said, and contrived a yawn. 'I'll sleep now, and take heart from your words... will you come again?'

'I would be glad to,' Mattheus said. 'My dear Yorick...' He rose and moved to the door. There he turned briefly, smiled at me and was gone.

That night, the ghost that came was Gitte.

There was no mist, no slow appearance of her shape out of the gloom. She came as a livid flame, the mad-eyed mother of Yorick's boyhood, bearing down upon him like a fury who would claw him to pieces where he lay. And her first words were: 'What have you done, you worthless little turd?'

'Nothing, Mother,' I whimpered. 'I've done no wrong...'

'Liar! You've done naught but wrong since I left you. I should have had Edela put a curse on you – made your cock fall off, and serve you right.'

'I know I've been a rogue,' I protested feebly. 'I'll change, I swear-'

'You won't!' Gitte snarled. 'You wretch - I'll curse you myself, turn you into a worm. Then a bird will eat you up, turn you into shit as you deserve.'

'Please don't,' I begged. 'I'm to read the bible... the priest has faith in me...'

'Him?' She gave a wild laugh. 'He thinks you're accursed! Have you lost your senses? You should trust no-one – even King Rorik himself.'

'Rorik's dead, Mother…'

'I've seen him, and he says you disappoint him. He would geld you, like he promised.'

'Will you ask him not to?' I implored. 'Or I'll never make you a grandmother…'

'You? You'll never be a father – you're unfit!' Gitte cried. 'Better throw yourself from the window, like the one you drove to it. Have you forgotten her?'

'No… I never have and never will,' I said, as tears welled. 'I loved her…'

But there was a rush of wind, a blinding light… in desperation I reached out – and awoke thrashing about on my pallet, with sunlight stabbing my eyes and swallows diving outside the window. With a yelp I rolled on my side, clutched the coverlet and buried my face in it, seeking only darkness. It was some time before I moved, roused by a thud on the door followed by the arrival of a maid bearing a platter and a mug; it was Thura.

'Waited on like a lord now, are we?' She sneered. 'Best enjoy it while it lasts, I'd say.' Having placed her wares on the floor, she stood regarding me with contempt.

'To think I once let you touch me,' she said, and went.

The night following that, when I'd not stirred from my pallet all day, another ghost came which at last forced me into action; it was Runa.

At first I was unaware of her presence, until a voice I knew spoke softly in my ear. I turned sharply to see her face close to mine - and she was smiling.

'Dearest Runa…' I tried to reach out, but could not move.

'My would-be rescuer,' she murmured. 'I know you tried.'

'I did, I swear…' tears blurred my vision. 'And I would have tried again – why did you leave me?'

'To seek a way out, of course. A way for us both.'

'But how would I find you?'

'You know how,' Runa said.

'I don't… will you show me?'

'You must flee, as I told you to,' was her reply. 'You're not safe where you are – you must know that.'

'But I'm confined… I'm sick…'

'You're clever. You'll find a way.'

She was fading. And though I begged her to stay, she shrank away. I called her name, but to no avail. Soon she was gone... and this time when I awoke it was dark and chill, with a pale moon showing through the casement.

I sat up, breathing hard. Then, throwing aside the coverlet I got to my feet, going first to the window and peering out: all was still, not even a night-bird calling. I went to the door and would have tried the latch, but hesitated: what was it I feared - that it was barred from without, or even guarded? I cursed myself for a clod, standing shivering in the gloom, and took hold of the handle. It lifted, whereupon the door was soon open and I was on the threshold, peering along the deserted passage - and at last, I made a decision.

Runa was right: I must flee while I could. And Gitte was right: I should trust no-one. And Makan was right: if I stayed here any longer, I would fall into madness. I cast off my shroud of idleness and misery, and sprang to action.

All I felt now was a sense of urgency; there was no time to reflect. Quickly I dressed, found my shoes and my belt with purse attached, almost empty though it was. I would take nothing more: I must move light and swift as a fugitive – for what else was I? Besides, there was nothing I valued save Makan's old shawm: in sadness I gazed at it, but knew it had to stay. With a last, fleeting glance about my chamber, I stepped outside.

There was no-one about the upper stories, nor on the stairs. With my pulse playing the tabor, creeping close to the walls like a thief, I gained the ground floor where I halted, ears straining for any sound. But I heard nothing... could it truly be this easy? Torches burned in their sconces, and somewhere outside a hound barked, but the way seemed clear: a turning, then another into the hallway that led to the presence chamber: I would not risk the main entrance, but hurry to the side door that led to the garden and stable-yard. After that...

I dared not think what came after that; somehow, I must evade the sentries and find a place where I could scale the walls. If fortune favoured me, I could take the path down to the Sund: there was moonlight enough, and there were boats...

I froze once, hearing footsteps, but they were some way off: a guard at his post, stamping on the stones. Soon I was moving again, hugging the walls... until a voice brought me to a stop. Inching forward, I peered around the corner, then drew back: by the turning to the main passage two guards sat on stools, sharing a jug. The way was blocked.

It was my worst moment, or so I thought. There was no other way out, nor was going back a choice. Hence, I saw only one solution: the Yorick of old, who once roamed the castle by night because he couldn't sleep, must revive his habit - and make others believe he had.

He was on.

'What, my bucks - carousing on duty?' I said, rounding the corner and stopping in apparent surprise. As both men jumped to their feet, I wagged a finger. 'Lucky it's me who caught you, or you'd be in deep shit, eh?'

'By the gods, Yorick,' one of them breathed. 'You shouldn't frit a man like that.'

'Serves you right,' I grinned. 'What's it worth, then, to persuade me to be on my way without seeing you?'

'Where are you going?' The other asked. 'I heard you were too sick to leave your bed.'

'I'm mending,' I told him. 'Need to get some air... I've been caged like a rat, and must stretch myself.'

But both men looked uneasy. 'Do you have leave from the physician?' The first one asked.

'Better than that,' I told him. 'I have leave from the priest, to go to the chapel and pray for my recovery. Me and Father Mattheus, we're bosom friends.'

At that, the two of them were about to laugh – which was the turning-point I needed.

'How dare you scoff!' I assumed my outraged face. 'I'm in earnest as always... and more, there's no kitchen wench waiting outside to tug my cock. I deny it – I deny everything. Now, do I get a drink of what's in that jug before I go? I've a mighty thirst. I might even fall into a fit, and make a lot of noise...'

'You're a whoreson rogue, Yorick,' the first guard muttered; but there was a smile trying to get out. 'Here, take a mouthful and no more.'

He held out the jug, and I lost no time in accepting his offer. It was watered mead, but I'd have drunk if it were horse piss. Wiping my lips, I returned it.

'I'll demand another on my way back,' I warned, and was gone.

A moment later I was unbolting a side door and stepping outside. I paused only to pull it shut, then stumbled along the pathways towards the eastern wall. It was almost over: freedom lay ahead, and what a powerful thought that was. I reached the stable wall, passed beyond it – and stopped at sight of a burning brazier, with a figure standing beside it. The sentry looked up at once, but I knew he would not catch me; I drew breath and was about to sprint the remaining distance to the wall... somehow, I would find a niche and clamber up...

That's when a hand, heavy as a great paw, landed on my shoulder. With a yelp I turned... to find a poniard levelled at my throat.

'You shouldn't be abroad, Master Yorick,' a calm voice said. In terror I looked up into the face of one of the King's guards, tall and battle-ready as always.

'You'll catch a chill,' he added. 'Let me help you indoors, and back to your bed.'

Thereafter Yorick was indeed a prisoner; and he remains so yet.

TWENTY-THREE

Mattheus brought paper and ink, so that I could write.

My first, most urgent wish was to address Prince Hamlet, begging him to visit me. I was unsure how to pen it, never having written a real letter before, so I kept it short. I spoke of my sickness, believing that was what others had told him, but assured him I was recovering and most desirous to see him, if only for a short while. I signed it *your loving servant and playfellow Yorick,* drew the tail of the last letter into a serpent and labelled it Jofurr, which I thought he would like. After folding it carefully and tying it with a lace pulled from my breeches, I waited for Mattheus's next appearance before handing it to him.

'I will be your messenger, and deliver it,' he said. 'Though I fear it's of little use. The King and Queen will never allow him to come here, for fear of infection.'

'But I'm not sick,' I said for perhaps the fifth time. 'You know it as well as I...'

I stopped myself; since the night of my Attempted Escape such protestations had been useless. I still shuddered when I recalled the way I'd been marched back indoors and up the stairs, and the looks I received from the sentries I'd cozened. Thereafter I was clapped up like a felon, my only comfort being that I was spared imprisonment in Helsingor's fearful dungeon. As I've told, my door had no lock – but a guard was now posted outside, day and night. It was he who placed my meagre breakfasts and suppers on the floor, and emptied my pail of its slops; no maid came, not even Thura. Nor did anyone else come - except Mattheus. What a turnabout that was: from being someone I had once derided, he had become the one I eagerly awaited.

'Have you tried to read the holy book?' He asked, pulling me from my tangled thoughts. 'I'm certain that if you do, you will find comfort.'

He was sitting before the window on my joined stool, hands in his lap. I opened my mouth, thinking to rebuff him, but curbed the notion; he was my only friend, and must be nurtured with care. Summoning my contrite face, I shook my head. The bible lay beside my pallet, unopened since he'd left it.

'In truth, comfort seems a foreign land to me now,' I said forlornly. 'I know not what to do, save to petition for my release. I've done no crime, have I? Save lifting a little food and drink, I mean. If I could only stand before the King and plead my case... I believe he's a just man, who would listen.'

Mattheus was silent for a while, then: 'I fear he would not, Yorick.'

I looked sharply at him, his figure dark against the sunlight that streamed in.

'The Queen speaks against you,' he went on. 'There's been talk of banishment. In truth...' He paused, then: 'The truth is harsh and may dismay you, but I'll tell it if you wish.'

'I do wish,' I said, with a frown coming on.

'It's believed you're a madman, and unfit to walk abroad. You could be a danger to others – especially the Prince.'

I froze, feeling my heart sink to depths yet unplumbed. A madman... then it struck me like a blow: this was how Gertrude would destroy me! What need had she of poison? As it was, most thought me a reckless fool: what could be simpler than shutting me away until I died? Alas, poor Yorick, they would say; lost his wits and had to be confined for his own good... such a waste...

I gazed up at Mattheus, who wore a look of pity. 'I see only one course open to you now,' he said. 'To repent of your dissolute ways, ask to be baptised into our mother church, and make full confession of your sins. If that were done, I might speak to the King and Queen on your behalf.'

But my mind was whirling. Mattheus, I guessed, did not know that Gertrude wished me dead. Banishment alone would not serve her ends, since that would leave me free to spill her secret...

'If I were to write to the King, would you carry that message for me?' I asked.

Hearing that, he was uncomfortable. 'Would that not seem an affront, given your case? And besides, what could you say that is new to him?'

'That I'm unjustly held prisoner,' I said quickly. 'That I'm in health, and pine for company – and most of all, to sport with my beloved Prince. That I desire only to prove myself worthy... to sing for him, perhaps.'

'You must let me think upon it,' Mattheus said. Brisk on a sudden, he stood up. 'But I will take your letter to the Prince. Is there aught else you need?'

'Couldn't smuggle a maid in, could you?' I asked; a feeble attempt at a jest. 'I'm not fussy which one.' But when he frowned, I begged his pardon. He started for the door, then stopped.

'What if you were to write a tract of repentance?'

Nonplussed, I stared at him.

'That would be a worthy task, would it not – and a wholesome one.'

He was smiling. 'It would keep you busy from morn 'til night – stop your mind from wandering into dark places. Many a man has found peace and contentment from such. I think of the great Augustine and his Confessions - I could lend you my copy. And while you labour, I could make it known what you do... would that not bring hope to everyone, even the Queen?'

'But that could take weeks, or even months,' I said, aghast. 'Moreover, I can't spell properly-'

'I could help you.'

'But what would I repent of? I've done no crime, unless fooling and fucking be-'

'Yorick, enough!' He regarded me with a pained look. 'Do I truly need to define sin for you? You know what's what – as you also know how folk regard you.'

I opened my mouth, but he held up a hand.

'Think, I pray you. Survey your life from earliest memories, and search your heart - you know what is there, while I cannot.' He paused, then: 'Think of it as another letter, if you will – a letter to yourself, if not to the Lord above. Honesty and humility must be your watchwords – for who can a man be honest with, if not himself? As for the Lord: you cannot lie to Him, who sees and knows everything.'

Confiteo: I was dumbstruck. The notion filled me with foreboding, as if I'd been set to hard labour. It dismayed me too – and on a sudden, it irked me.

'So - this is my penance, is it?' I asked sourly.

He made no reply.

'Payment for my wicked ways,' I went on, my anger rising. 'And a means of keeping me mewed up here until I'm forgotten.'

'It was but a suggestion,' Mattheus answered. 'The choice, of course, is yours.'

'You smug weasel!' I shouted then. 'You pious, whey-faced turd! You come as one doing charity - visiting a deluded fool who's lost his wits, who knows not truth from chaff! I served a King who trusted me - who counted on me! I was cheered to the rafters once - paid in gold! Why should you judge me?'

'I never judge,' Mattheus said, speaking softly. 'Only God can do that.'

He turned from me and went out without looking back. I heard him exchange words with the guard, who seized the latch and slammed the door; the thud fell on my ears like the Crack of Doom.

And yet, here was another turnabout.

Two days later Mattheus came again, to tell me there was no answer from Prince Hamlet; and more, that I was not permitted to send further letters to him. Whereupon, having racked his brains for the past two nights to find a resolution, Yorick fell on his knees and begged the priest to let him write his repentance tract, which would be the outpourings of his very soul, no matter how long it took, and may God help him or strike him dead. And more, if Mattheus could find it in his heart to forgive him for the hard words he had uttered, and the way he'd cursed and insulted him, he would be in his debt for the rest of his days, and Yorick was the most wretched and unworthy fool in all of Denmark. And if…

Through all of which Mattheus gaped, before putting his hands to his ears and crying out for me to stop.

'By all the saints, Yorick,' he breathed. 'Of course you're forgiven, and of course I don't think you unworthy... what in heaven made you think so?'

And at the look of sympathy on his face, I wept: real tears, which seemed to bring a tear to his own eye. But *confiteo*: how different it could have been, had he known Yorick well - the Yorick who had another purpose in mind entirely.

I'd not been a player for nothing – and I would not fail to deceive even him. If I was to remain a prisoner here, I would endure it for the present – for I had made a decision: to write my True Tale - my true testimony, leaving nothing out. I would keep it private, insisting Mattheus read not a word until it was done, only asking him how to spell certain words. When it was finished, I would beg for admission to his church so that I could make confession of my sins.

Whereupon, as soon as I found myself trusted enough to walk outdoors, I would make my escape from Helsingor, even if it killed me.

TWENTY-FOUR

Confiteo: my mind isn't what it was.

It is not because the *mareridt* comes often, for it seldom does. Nor is it because the ghosts berate me as they used to - Makan, Gitte, even Huginn once – for they no longer do so; they have abandoned me like everyone else. I penned no more letters after the one to the Prince was ignored; I know not if he even saw it. How could I, confined in my chamber which is now my cell? I'm like a ghost too, I recall thinking once. All I have is my Tale: the task which is both my trial and my salvation; my trial, because it has been the hardest thing I ever did. And my salvation, because without it I would have lost all hope and become a true madman, fit to roam the forests like a beast and howl at the moon. Someone once told me of a boy who did that... I forget who.

I believe I've spent seven or eight months on my Tale, though it could even be nine – a fitting number, since it comes to full term soon, ready to emerge into the world. Though of course, it cannot – emerge, I mean – for none must see it until I'm far away from here, and safe. Then, and only then, will it be known what passed: how the King of Denmark was betrayed by his wife and his brother - and is so yet, for all I know. Mayhap after he's gone, his ghost will seek revenge for that treachery: the secret that was known to a very few. And they are all dead now - save Yorick. Or so I believe...

I ask Mattheus for news, but he tells me little. Nor does he come so often as he did, chiefly to see how goes my Repentance Tract... but do I speak of Repentance? A pox and a plague on that, and on the priest and his piety! When I'm done, and my Tale is read, he'll be seen for what he is: an innocent, whose knees must be worn to the bone with praying – for Yorick's soul! Could anyone think of a greater waste of time? I would scorn him now - but I do not. He is an ambassador from the world outside, and my only friend... see, I stray again.

In truth my Tale is almost done, yet I dare not tell Mattheus for he would ask to see it. He has already, many times, but I refuse him, clutching the sheaf of papers to my chest as though it were my child. I've sworn I will show them when I've penned my last word - though what that might be I do not know, save that it shall not be Amen.

Denmark's a prison. And I'll speak now of the time since I was confined, even if the memory has faded somewhat. I remember I once tried to flee, but was caught by a man with a poniard. Thereafter I was a prisoner - and in mortal fear of being poisoned. Yet I was mistaken there, for how easy it would have been for the Queen – who still wants me dead, I'll swear – to have my food tainted with some noxious substance, in quantities I could not taste, until I expired? Easy enough, and yet I live… and it seems I have Mattheus to thank for it.

'She rejoices to hear of how you're altered, Yorick,' he used to say. 'As she does when I tell of your reading the holy book. The King too, though I see less of him: a campaigner always, who prepares for war.' He would assume one of his sad little smiles. 'Blessed are the peacemakers, our Saviour said; I will never cease to pray that the King comes to that view one day…'

'But what of the Prince?' I would interrupt, ever eager for tidings of my beloved boy. 'Does he ride? Does he fence, and tilt at the quintain as he wished to do?' And once, somewhat absently, I asked: 'How old is he now?'

'Prince Hamlet is seven years of age,' Mattheus answered.

At that I gave a start and peered at my window, though in truth it was so grimed that I could barely tell if it were day or night.

'Is winter gone, then? I thought it was Yule…'

'Yuletide is long past, Yorick,' Mattheus said, with a pitying smile. 'And I regret I must leave you now. Is there aught you need? More ink, paper or…?'

I was uneasy: something had been troubling me, and I feared that I might forget to speak of it. On seeing my expression he paused, whereupon I voiced it.

'There's a service I must ask, Father Mattheus,' I began; I've long since called him Father. 'It concerns my burial... if I should die before my time, that is.'

'What, do you fear that you might?' Mattheus lifted his brows in that way he has. 'Surely not. You are infirm, but it will pass... I pray for your recovery every day. These are morbid thoughts - turn to the book, as I do, and find comfort.'

'It's the King I would turn to,' I said, 'but I cannot. And hence, it's he I would beg you to speak to.'

Whereupon I told him of how King Rorik promised I would be interred in the sanctified graveyard where kings and nobles lie, as my mother once hoped. And how Gertrude annulled the order after her father's death, and how it had preyed on me ever since, and...'

'I understand.' Mattheus held up a hand. 'You, who were valued and trusted by Rorik... some would say you deserve such. So long as your death is natural.' He smiled. 'Let me importune our King's good counsellor, when I judge the time is right. I'm sure Polonius will listen – he asked after you, but a few days back. Does that not give you hope?'

It did, I told him. Then, as a notion occurred: 'You once thought me bewitched, did you not?'

He made a slight movement... I might call it a shudder. 'I told you I did not believe it,' he reminded me.

He moved to the door. 'I did ask the King's physician to come to you, as I promised. Yet he has fallen victim to this ague that infects Helsingor... others are sick, like you. But our prayers will be answered, and it will pass.'

And he was gone. Whereupon I reached for my board, my paper and inkhorn, and began to scratch away once again.

Last night, I finished the last of the holy wine.

Have I spoken of it already? If I have, *me ignosce* – that means 'forgive me' in Latin; Mattheus taught it me... or perhaps it was Polonius, but no matter. The precious drink - a deep-red, somewhat bitter wine - was brought to me in secret by Mattheus some days ago, hidden under his robes. He made an unlikely conspirator, being ashamed of his own action: sneaking the flagon past the guard, I mean. Once inside, he bade me conceal it and drink only sparingly, for it would be the only one he dared bring; a mouthful at morning, perhaps, and another at night – I should think of it as physic. It would soothe my stomach, he said, since it had grown troublesome of late. It's true I'm weak; I can barely rise to use the tin jordan. Now I keep it close by, and seldom rise at all. This dismays me: I must regain full use of my body, or else how will I get down the stairs, let alone make my escape?

My mind is not what it was.

Today I slept a good deal. I'll soon write no more, for there's naught left to tell - save that I dreamed of Runa. She was unhappy, begging me to flee to her as I should have done long ago... I implored her to be patient. As she faded, I thought I heard her singing.

But when will Hamlet come? I wrote to him, yet he never answered. Does he even remember me? I miss him more than I can bear: our games and frolics, Yorick as his charger bearing him on his back to the kitchens, where the maids gathered about him... what does he do now? I wonder. Does he still fall into melancholy, and talk to himself? It troubles me - for who else can lift his humour, as Yorick did? Who else will gambol with him, and play at animals, and make jests about Polonius? Will he ever kiss these parched and scabbed lips of mine now? I fear not... I fear his gorge would rise at the thought.

As for Gertrude: I have denied her. I have ordered myself to outlive her – on pain of death! I still chuckle to recall that, though it sets me to coughing... no matter. My ink will run out soon, and I must think on how to hide my book. When I'm free of this ague Mattheus speaks of... when I can go about again... when I can take a cup of good Rhenish...

I dreamed of the hex Edela today, and she spoke of Gitte.

'She cut her own fingers off, did you not know?' She told me. 'Buried them, as a sacrifice. She was barren and prayed for a daughter... she got you instead. Perhaps you'll meet her again. And another thing: the wine is poisoned – you shouldn't have trusted the churchman.'

She drifted away then, leaning on her stick. And as she went, she murmured something I barely heard. It sounded like *Remember: he who buries you, will dig you up...*

I awoke, angry and shaking... a pox on her, I say. A cruel accusation, to level at the man who has been my comforter for what seems an age. The age of Yorick...

Confiteo: that's Latin for 'I confess'. It's how I'm advised to begin my Tale, in the manner of a confession. Though I forget what... I'm somewhat weak for writing more ... and now come voices I must go.

POSTREMO

By God's grace and with due humility I, Counsellor to the King of Denmark, pen this private testimony of my own free will, to the purpose of laying forth how I carried out his orders in respect of the disposal of the person of his jester. May my words remain with Yorick's book, in a safe place bespoken by him, for being so enfeebled he could not take it with him. Let it lie there until such time as I am retired from office, and am at leisure to retrieve it.

At Yorick's request, I have not read it. *Hic Juro*: this I swear.

Hear then how I took him at nightfall from his foul chamber – or rather a servant did so at my behest, on payment of a hundred *pennings* for his silence and promise of a safe passage from Helsingor to wherever he pleased. Yorick, a veritable wraith in rags, was wrapped in a shroud and borne from the castle, slung over the man's back like a sack of grain; he was so shrunken he could pass as a corpse. Thereafter he was conveyed to a secluded place outside the castle walls, freed from his shroud, given a sum of money and left to make his way to such destination as he chose on condition he never returned.

This, I swear, was done at the King's behest, for my sovereign lord would not let his poor fool die alone and abed as, for reasons unknown, the Queen intended.

Our parting was brief; he was silent as I had never known him – and yet I make bold to declare that there remained a faint gleam in his eye, that spoke of a spirit yet undimmed. May good fortune go with him, I said; in truth, for all his dissolute ways I could not find it in my heart to condemn my onetime *vexator*, who loved his master Prince Hamlet and would have given his life for him.

I come now to the darkest part of my testimony, which I like not, but it being by my sovereign's order, it was carried out to the fullest extent. Know then that, following Yorick's departure, the corpse of a poor soul who had perished outside

Helsingor – a wandering pedlar, stricken by some sickness – was shrouded and trussed and delivered to the graveyard that same night, to be interred the following morning as the King's loyal jester, among the highborn of Denmark. Absalom the sexton received the body with due humility, saying he would give his friend Yorick the finest burial a man could have. Though mark this: I have a suspicion that, as I left him, I saw a smile play about the fellow's lips, before it was quickly suppressed.

Father Mattheus, the Queen's chaplain, conducted the ceremony with due reverence, and many were the folk of Helsingor who came at last to bear witness.

This is what was done. May the Lord have mercy on us all henceforth, and on the soul of Yorick, wherever he may be.

Humbly do I take my leave: Polonius, *consiliarius regis*.
Finis.

Printed in Great Britain
by Amazon